SHELTERS FROM THE STORMS OF

ANXIETY, DEPRESSION AND STRESS

JOE S. BEAN, PH.D.

BALBOA.
PRESS
A DIVISION OF HAY HOUSE

The information, ideas, and suggestions in this book are not intended as a substitute for professional advice. Before following any suggestions contained in this book, you should consult your personal physician or mental health professional. Neither the author nor the publisher shall be liable or responsible for any loss or damage allegedly arising as a consequence of your use or application of any information or suggestions in this book.

Balboa Press books may be ordered through booksellers or by contacting:

Balboa Press
A Division of Hay House
1663 Liberty Drive
Bloomington, IN 47403
www.balboapress.com
1 (877) 407-4847

Because of the dynamic nature of the Internet, any web addresses or links contained in this book may have changed since publication and may no longer be valid. The views expressed in this work are solely those of the author and do not necessarily reflect the views of the publisher, and the publisher hereby disclaims any responsibility for them.

The author of this book does not dispense medical advice or prescribe the use of any technique as a form of treatment for physical, emotional, or medical problems without the advice of a physician, either directly or indirectly. The intent of the author is only to offer information of a general nature to help you in your quest for emotional and spiritual well-being. In the event you use any of the information in this book for yourself, which is your constitutional right, the author and the publisher assume no responsibility for your actions.

Any people depicted in stock imagery provided by Getty Images are models, and such images are being used for illustrative purposes only. Certain stock imagery © Getty Images.

Print information available on the last page.

ISBN: 978-1-9822-3285-6 (sc)
ISBN: 978-1-9822-3286-3 (e)

Balboa Press rev. date: 08/13/2019

CONTENTS

I. INTRODUCTION

II. FEATURED TOPICS: ANXIETY, DEPRESSION, AND STRESS

ANXIETY

DEPRESSION

STRESS

DEDICATION

Shelters from The Storms of Anxiety, Depression and Stress was inspired by my beloved parents, Joe and Mary Bean, my children, Jacob, Joey and Samantha Bean, my brother, Jere Bean, and clients who have benefited from my counseling services. Special thanks to Samantha Bean who helped me with the editing process.

PREFACE

This is the ultimate self-help book for weathering the "storms" of anxiety, depression and stress because the author presents a clear, complete and concise approach to the "storms" that excludes unnecessary filler material. Since anxiety, depression and stress exist in varying degrees within all persons, most anyone can benefit from reading this user-friendly book.

As a therapy tool for clients, the book reflects the notion that "knowledge is power" and therefore assists them with their therapeutic goals. Therapists can integrate much of the material into sessions that use bibliotherapy in combination with psychotherapy. Psychology and counseling professors can use the book as supplemental reading for certain courses. The general reader can use it as a guide for living in a productive manner.

RESILIENCE: THE HEART OF MENTAL HEALTH

Resilience, willpower and emotional intelligence are infused into curative guidelines for correcting disordered thoughts, feelings and behaviors.

Resilience lies at the heart of mental health because it allows you to "bounce back" from hard times and possibly become stronger in the process as you learn to endure negative events while relentlessly pursuing life goals. Resiliency enables you to recall what you have learned from negative experiences, remind yourself of how you overcame setbacks, and realize that most life stressors are temporary (Flach,1997).

Resiliency coaches you to see difficult times in terms of the Swahili Warrior Song message that: "Life has meaning only in the struggle. Triumph or defeat is in the hands of the gods. So, let us celebrate the struggle."

THE STEELING OF RESILIENCE WITH WILLPOWER

Willpower refers to the amount of self-control you have as you alternate between comfort and stretch zones (McGonigal, 2012). Choose your willpower battles wisely because the body needs time to recover after exercising a significant amount of self-control. When stretching your comfort zones, select slightly more difficult options each day. (Baumeister & Tierney, 2011).

You need to be extremely alert for occasions when you could deceive yourself into thinking that you deserve rewards that go against your willpower goals. When you deceive yourself, you shift power away from your evolved thinking brain into the clutches of your reward-seeking, impulsive, primitive brain which thrives on a powerful neurotransmitter known as dopamine. Anything that you think will make you feel good triggers a release of dopamine.

Although you need the promise of reward to keep you motivated on tasks, separate dopamine rewards that give your life meaning from those that distract you from your life goals (McGonigal, 2012).

If you expand space and time distances when you crave something, power shifts to the control of your thinking brain. Space distancing increases the amount of space between you and an unneeded reward, while time distancing extends elapsed time before you indulge in the reward.

During an unsuccessful attempt to reduce a craving, you may say "what the hell" and violate your values instead of taking the proper course of thinking about how a relapse happened, forgiving yourself and therefore breaking the self-destructive "what-the-hell" cycle. When a tempting thought comes to mind, accept the thought and let it pass on by as you would while watching a train thunder into the night. If you wait your cravings out, they will pass in due time (McGonigal, 2012).

EMOTIONAL INTELLIGENCE

Your emotional intelligence (EQ) is measured by how you develop relationships, manage your emotions, and continually improve the quality of your personal and social skills. On an interpersonal level, a high EQ trumps a high IQ every time because no one cares how smart you are if you make others feel uncomfortable (Goleman, 2005).

Your EQ can be broken down into five components:

1. Self-Awareness. This component refers to your ability to think through your emotions and put your strong points in motion. You accurately assess your strengths, limitations and how others react to you, refrain from bragging and gossiping, and realize how your emotions make an impact on others.

In increasing your self-awareness, remind yourself that emotions exist in order to help you understand something important about yourself and others. You need to tolerate some emotional discomfort in order to sort things out and deal with issues in constructive ways.

2. Self-Management. As a self-manager, you do not make rushed decisions and you refuse to stereotype or attack others. You adapt well to change and take responsibility for your actions. When someone frustrates you, you keep your composure and respond to that person with your thinking brain.

3. Internal Motivation. This component allows you to see activities as opportunities to build your potential by learning more about topics.

As you develop the curiosity and energy to attain possible goals, internal motivation impels you to become involved in challenging activities, whether you work on cars, weed gardens, read books, write stories, jog, and so on.

4. Empathy. In order to be empathic, you need to "walk in the shoes of others" and ask yourself "How would I feel if I were in this situation?" Empathy requires quick recognition of the wants, needs and viewpoints of others as you gauge their words, emotions, and body language. You actively listen to the tone, speech and volume of their voices and look for messages that may exist below the surface of their spoken words.

5. Social Skills. This EQ component involves relationship management strategies that take time, effort and asking yourself questions like:

Am I likable and easy to talk to?
Do I treat people with respect?
Am I a good listener who can help others build their hopes and dreams?
Can I apologize when I am too intense?
Do I live by the values that I believe to be correct?

The more you show interest in others' stories, the better you interpret their needs correctly. In order to build social skills most effectively, remember that trust is difficult to build, easy to lose, and often ends up being your most difficult relationship management goal (Goleman, 2005).

ANXIETY, EXISTENTIAL LIVING, MINDFULNESS AND ANXIETY DISORDERS

Disordered Anxiety Versus Productive Anxiety

Unlike disordered anxiety, productive anxiety creates awareness that you need to become "high" on struggling for self-fulfillment and appreciating the good choices you have made. Existential anxiety is a type of productive anxiety that alerts you to your need to accomplish as many goals as possible in order to make your short existence on earth an exciting, daring adventure.

The "Four Horsemen" Of Existential Living

The "four horsemen of the apocalypse" represented in the Bible are construed in existential living as the "four horsemen" of death awareness, freedom to make choices, isolation, and the search for meaning in life. If you fail to make appropriate choices in any of these areas, you will most likely experience disordered anxiety (Yalom, 1980).

1. Death Awareness. Death awareness involves learning to deal with growing older, divorcing, losing relatives, friends, and jobs as well as

seeing your children grow up and not seem to need you that much anymore.

Death awareness events serve to make you focus on your need to stay busy and recollect how you have survived many chaotic times. Continual awareness of your impending death can also encourage you to make meaningful decisions and form a childlike appreciation for beautiful sunsets, rainbows, outings with family and friends, and all the other simple things in life.

2. Freedom to Make Choices. This "horseman" represents your call of duty to make responsible choices. If you experience making choices with a sense of dread, you may endeavor to escape responsibility by either allowing others to make your decisions or waiting until you are forced by circumstances to make "eleventh hour" choices. (Fromm, 1994).

3. Isolation. No one can be born for you or die for you. You need to balance out solitude with togetherness and a spiritual life in order to be empowered enough to turn loneliness into a healthy form of solitude.

4. Meaning. While short-term meaning comes from being engaged in a career, raising a family, moving to a treasured home, and so forth, deeper meaning comes from "peak experiences" involving the feeling of awe that comes from witnessing life from a spiritual perspective (Yalom,1980).

Mindfulness

Mindfulness is an extreme state of self-awareness that helps you enjoy peak experiences in the here-and-now. With mindfulness, you act as an observer of your mind's random chatter, notice sensitive issues, and let potential stressors pass on by until you have time to deal with them.

The state of mindfulness prompts you to remember the Buddhist phrase, "rule your mind or your mind will rule you." In building mindful awareness, remember the following line from a film entitled The Samaritan: "If you keep on doing what you have always done, you will keep on being what you have always been. Nothing changes until you make it change."

Anxiety Disorders

Anxiety disorders have recently replaced depressive disorders as the most common mental disorders in the United States. The summary below presents the five anxiety disorders.

1. Generalized Anxiety Disorder. People with generalized anxiety experience free-floating worry and muscle tension. Although victims of generalized anxiety are restless, easily startled, and prone to sleep problems, they can usually perform social and work activities. This disorder affects women and the impoverished twice as often as males and those with higher incomes.

2. Panic Disorder. Panic-disordered persons experience unexpected panic attacks that usually peak within ten minutes and possibly occur for no apparent reason. Panic disorder may trigger a concomitant condition known as agoraphobia in which you become fearful of going far from home, usually because you dread having a panic attack in some dangerous or embarrassing situation.

3. Social Anxiety Disorder. This disorder involves a chronic, irrational fear of embarrassment and/or humiliation in social situations. The social fear may be narrow, such as fear of making speeches, or involve a broad-based dread of inadequate social functioning. People with social anxiety often judge their social and work performances too harshly.

4. Specific Phobia. This intense fear is limited to certain objects or situations. Specific fears often revolve around animals (zoophobia), arachnids (arachnophobia), insects (entomophobia), heights

(acrophobia), flying (aerophobia), snakes (ophidiophobia), water (hydrophobia), and blood (hematophobia).

5. Obsessive-Compulsive Disorder. Obsessions are thoughts that intrude into your mind while compulsions are unproductive actions that temporarily relieve anxiety caused by obsessions. For example, cleaning is a compulsion designed to relieve the fear of contamination, checking is a compulsion that aims at removing doubts, and arranging is a compulsion that aims to restore order in your life.

ANXIETY AND SELF-ESTEEM

Anxiety, Fears and Behaviors of People with Low Self-Esteem

Anxiety reduces your self-esteem because it limits your ability to bounce back after disappointments, learn from mistakes, make good choices, and develop new skills. Until you are able to conquer anxiety, you will go through life feeling fearful, disappointed, always on guard for criticism, and being unable to relax (Southwick & Charney, 2012).

If you have low self-esteem, your anxiety may build to the point that you continually seek reassurance from others and may become hounded by fears such as:

1. Fear of doing something that will make you feel inadequate
2. Fear that you will be humiliated again
3. Fear that you will lose self-respect
4. Fear that you will never be successful
5. Fear that you will be rejected

Behaviors of people with low self-esteem include:

1. Trying to please others
2. Extreme defensiveness when criticized

3. Giving up easily or working hard to cover up weaknesses
4. Being shy and passive around others
5. Avoiding potentially embarrassing situations
6. Beating themselves up on a regular basis
7. Neglecting or abusing themselves

How to Raise Your Self-Esteem

1. Lighten up- don't take yourself so seriously.
2. If you keep feeling sorry for yourself, others will lose patience with you.
3. See your mistakes as lessons that will improve you.
4. Pressure yourself to enter uncertain situations and make new friends.
5. Be assertive. Don't say "yes" when you want to say "no."
6. Explore yourself, take risks and do things that you have not done before.
7. Take good care of your health. Exercise improves your mood and your self-esteem. Getting enough sleep and good food are necessary for having a positive outlook and energy you need in times of stress.
8. Respect yourself for who you are. Remind yourself of your strengths and any progress you have made.
9. Look for evidence before you take negative thoughts at face value. Discover factual support for your self-worth and be able to laugh at your mistakes (Bourne, 2010).

Some Self-Esteem Building Activities

Reading, which allows you to escape, meditate and process things better.

Walking, especially near water, which ionizes the air and relaxes you.

Exercising, which replaces bad thoughts with good thoughts about getting healthier Counting your strengths, blessings, and being patient with yourself

Cap these activities off by reciting the Serenity Prayer: "God grant me the serenity to accept things I cannot change, courage to change the things I can and wisdom to know the difference."

Healthy Self-Esteem Beliefs

I like the way I look.
I can finish anything I start.
I think people enjoy hanging out with me.
I think I have accomplished a lot in life.
I consider my reasoning ability to be adequate.

I can quickly get over feelings of guilt or shame.
I don't beat myself up when I make mistakes.
I feel worthwhile.
I see most stressors as challenges, not threats.
I try to improve myself in some way each and every day.

I feel spiritually connected to a higher power.
I do not turn small problems into huge catastrophes.
I mindfully live in the present.
I am not jealous of other people's successes.

I don't seek immediate revenge when mistreated.
If things do not work out with my partner, I can be happy without my partner.
I don't compare myself to others.
Life is not just passing me by- I feel happy.
I care for others, but I don't let them drain my energy.

I can quickly let go of negative thoughts and feelings.
I do not overreact when I am blamed for something.
I check in with both my thinking brain and gut-felt intuitions when making decisions.
I know that if I don't fix my needs first, I will be too down and worn out to help others.
I not only deserve respect, I demand respect.

ANXIETY 3

COPING WITH ANXIETY-PRODUCING BELIEFS

In order to reduce anxiety, change your false, irrational beliefs that produce self-defeating automatic negative thoughts. In doing this, you decrease anxiety and develop more constructive ways to overcome related issues such as frustration, guilt, shame, irritability, and procrastination.

Irrational Beliefs Behind Automatic Negative Thoughts

Irrational beliefs remain in the background of everyday choices that you make and can lead to automatic negative thoughts that blind you to certain facts when are engaged in decision-making.

Examples of Irrational Beliefs (Reivich & Shatte, 2002).

1. Irrational Belief That You Are Defective. You don't allow others to know you very well because you fear that they will detect your flaws. You may people-please others in hopes that they will overlook your shortcomings.

2. Irrational Belief That You Will Be Abandoned. You assume that you could never be happy on your own and worry that your partner and

friends will lose interest in you. You may keep digging for reassurance from others in order to feel loved and accepted.

3. Irrational Belief That You Need to Be Responsible for Practically Everything. You may exhaust yourself by needlessly going over what you need to do each day, take pride in covering each and every little chore and worry about making mistakes that would allow situations to get out of control.

4. Irrational Belief That You Are Helpless. You fret about not being able to take care of yourself and worry that you will not be happy if your partner leaves. You may remain in unrewarding jobs or relationships because you fear changes that might result in your feeling abandoned.

Coping Strategies

1. Systematically expose yourself to anxiety-provoking situations in order to decrease the intensity and frequency of your anxious beliefs.

2. You may limit your exposure to unpleasant situations, but you should not avoid them altogether because avoidance stifles growth experiences like special work meetings, going to weddings, graduations, dinners with relatives, and so forth.

3. Instead of complicating your life with multitasking, make your life simpler by finishing one thing at a time, starting with your most important priority.

4. Stay on a schedule that adds stability and security to your life. Make sure that regular sleep, balanced meals, and pleasurable activities are added to your "to do" list.

Positively Reframe Negative Self-Talk

When you reframe negative self-judgments, your positive self-talk shifts you into a better frame of mind. Such a shift can lead to attitudes that help you realize that, no matter what has happened in your life, you are not damaged goods and no one is better than you.

Positive reframing helps you see stressful situations as opportunities, not threats. It also encourages you to get the best out of life, stay in touch with your feelings and deal with problems in an open, honest manner (Neenan, 2009).

Some positive reframes are listed below.

Negative Attitude	Reframed Attitude
I am stubborn	I am determined
He wastes money	He is generous
He is bossy	He is a leader
I am too picky	I attend to detail
He won't follow rules	He is creative
She is fearful	She is cautious
She talks too much	She likes to share
She is nosy and interfering	She is concerned
This is a threatening problem	This is a challenge
I have anxiety attacks	I deal with them
I am crazy	I am irrational at times

ANXIETY 4

GENERALIZED (FREE-FLOATING) ANXIETY

Free-floating (generalized) anxiety involves uncontrollable anxiety and worry that drain your energy, keep your body tense, disrupt your sleep, impair your concentration, make you irritable and interfere with practically everything you do.

The negative emotions that push free-floating anxiety keep you worried about an unpredictable future. You over-think one "what-if" scenario after another and usually believe that something dreadful is going to happen. You may keep bringing anxiety-causing scenarios into your worried mind until you find yourself on a "dead-end street" of more worries.

Behavioral symptoms of generalized anxiety include:

A. Inability to relax, enjoy quiet time or feel comfortable while alone

B. Avoidance of situations that make you anxious

C. Procrastination with important decisions because you feel overwhelmed

D. An exaggerated startle response that makes you extremely sensitive to changes in your immediate environment.

Anger and Generalized Anxiety

1. Since emotions grounded in anxiety are often hard to express, you may try to power through them with anger. It is much better to check, catch and correct the fear or worry you are dealing with than to allow irresponsible anger outbursts to take over and possibly destroy some of your relationships.

2. You may use anger to give yourself more security over a situation. Examples: When you are going through a mental ritual of some sort to make yourself less anxious, you become angry when others distract you; if you are mentally rehearsing for a situation that makes you socially anxious, you snap at someone who interrupts your train of thought.

3. Anxiety and anger often pair up when you become a people-pleaser who complies with others' unwanted requests until you build up resentments that induce you to explode in anger.

4. Concern about rejection may blow a disagreement out of proportion if you conclude that your relationship has become threatened. Threat activates your brain's fight-or-flight response and leads you to body tension, racing thoughts, and irritability. Your restlessness about a relationship often limits effective communication with the involved person.

5.Your sensitive nature may make you worry that you cannot control the expression of your anger, so you may hold anger in check until you reach the point of having a hostile outburst.

6. Higher levels of anger often fuel the intensity of generalized anxiety disorder. Such anger can reduce the effectiveness of therapy for free-floating anxiety if the topic of irritability is not introduced into

treatment. A client needs to realize that powering through situations with anger is not a solution to anxiety.

Steps for Worry Management

1. Accept Your Worries. Accept the reality that you cannot control all life events. Acceptance allows you to direct your attention toward things you need to do and observe what is happening inside your head without judging yourself.

2. Do What Worries Have Made You Avoid. Tolerating some constructive discomfort can lead you to a sense of relief and pride.

3. Deep breathe as you consider whether anger is masking your anxiety over a situation.

4. Use the addition problem of 1 + 3 + 10 to control both anxiety and anger. One means to visualize a stop sign or red light and say to yourself "stop, calm down." Three means take three deep breaths as if you are swimming at the bottom of a swimming pool. Ten means to count from one to ten and back in military style- one thousand one, one thousand two, one thousand three, one thousand four, and so forth.

5. Sit in a comfortable chair with your arms unfolded. Take ten-second deep breaths as you count from one to ten and back, military style (1001, 1002, 1003, etc.) with eyes closed to avoid distractions. Decrease distractions further by visualizing mantras of the numbers from one to ten as you hold your breath and count. You will feel totally relaxed after several minutes of this practice.

6. Have A Set Worry Time.

A. Set a designated worry time to think about your problems.

B. Write down each worry as the day goes on and save it for your designated worry time.

C.If you catch yourself worrying outside of worry time, tell your brain, "not now, I have an appointment to think about this later."

D. Your brain will not accept force, but it will accept postponing your worries.

E. When worry time comes, think of possible solutions to each worry issue. Do not conduct worry time at night shortly before bedtime.

F. When you can perform this exercise well, you eliminate 23 hours and 30 minutes of undue worry (Leahy, R.L., 2005).

PANIC ATTACKS

Panic attacks include four or more of the following symptoms:

Out-of-control heart palpitations
Shaking
Breathing difficulties
A sense of choking
Nausea or stomach pain
Dizziness or light-headedness
Feeling like you are outside yourself or feeling unreal
Fearing that you are losing your mind
Fearing that you are dying
Experiencing numbness or tingling sensations
Chills or having hot flashes

The Role Of Adrenaline In Panic Attacks

There is no particular pattern to panic attacks. Some people experience several attacks a day, then have none for months, while others have attacks on a weekly basis. In any case, attacks occur when the body experiences a sudden surge of the stress hormone adrenaline that is out of proportion with any actual danger or threat.

When the nervous system acts normally to fear, adrenaline levels recede once a feared situation is removed, but adrenaline associated with panic attacks does not recede right away. Attacks normally last from 10-15 minutes, and full recovery from them can take several more minutes. Such attacks may be triggered by events, but some attacks come from "out-of-the-blue".

People who have frequent attacks often feel a need to be near an easy escape. They may end up avoiding crowds, bridges, leaving home alone or leaving home altogether. In such cases, panic disorder may be accompanied by agoraphobia. With severe cases of agoraphobia, a person's home becomes a type of prison where there is no social life and no chance of holding a typical job.

Amygdala: Your Fear Center

The almond-shaped fear center of the brain, the amygdala, reacts with a high-stress response to anxiety-producing life events or unfamiliar situations. Such catastrophic thinking involves thinking of worst-case scenarios- headaches become brain tumors, a pain in the chest means a heart attack is coming, or a noise in the middle of the night is interpreted as a burglar in the house.

Controlling the Symptoms of Panic Attacks

1. Knowledge Is Power. Know that panic attacks are simply amygdala misfires that cause surges of adrenaline. Even if panic attacks feel like heart attacks, they do not indicate a serious disease.

2. Deep-Breathe. Breathe slower, not faster, when a panic attack occurs. Use deep breaths to create a slow stream of air flow that prevents hyperventilation and a build-up of carbon dioxide in the blood.

3. Practice Mindfulness. Mindfulness controls catastrophic thinking as you catch thoughts before they can be blown out of proportion.

4. Exercise. Exercise encourages your body to produce natural, relaxing chemicals called endorphins that produce euphoria (a sense of well-being). Exercise also fosters relief from pain.

5. Eat Right. Alcohol and caffeine can trigger and/or worsen panic attacks. Never go more than four hours without eating and constantly check for dietary deficiencies. Carry a bottle of water to keep you hydrated and cool.

6. Do not confuse the heart pounding, difficulty breathing, chest discomfort, and light-headed, dizzy feelings of panic attacks with atrial fibrillation (A Fib). With A Fib, the emotional symptoms of panic (a feeling of unreality, fear of going crazy) are usually absent.

The irregular heartbeat symptoms of A Fib start and stop suddenly while the symptoms of panic attacks slowly return to normal rates. A Fib heartbeats change pace often while panic attack heartbeats are fast, but regular.

Final Thoughts on Panic Attacks

Accept panic attacks in the same way you would accept a headache- as a temporary nuisance that will pass. When you feel an attack coming on, try to buy yourself some time to fortify your composure and concentration. Deep breathe, stay in the present and avoid "what if" worrying. Try to resume what you were doing just before the panic attack.

Hyperventilation can be a causal factor with panic attacks because short, choppy breaths produce too much oxygen, drops in carbon dioxide levels and symptoms like dizziness, light-headedness, numbness, tingling, sweating, and shortness of breath. Remember to take in slow, deep breaths when you notice panic symptoms. Do not fight an attack- simply try to go about your business as much as possible during the course of the attack (Antony, M. & McCabe, R., 2004).

BUILDING COURAGE TO FACE SPECIFIC AND GENERAL FEAR

Specific Fears (Phobias)

Depending on their nature, specific fears may disturb your social and occupational functioning. Most fears can be desensitized through exposure therapy in which victims are gradually exposed to fearful situations until they are literally "bored" out of their respective fears. Some of the most socially and occupationally disabling phobias include:

Phonophobia: Noise or loud talking
Ochlophobia: Crowds
Xenophobia: Strangers
Ommatophobia: Eyes
Pogonophobia: Beards
Necrophobia: Corpses
Aerophobia: Flying
Hodophobia: Travel
Gephyrophobia: Crossing bridges
Ecclesiophobia: Churches

Some General Fears That Stifle Growth and Development

There are several fears that may stifle your dreams and prevent you from becoming all that you can become. Below, four of these fears are identified and explained.

Pain

Although too much pain can break you down, "no pain, no gain" means that enduring pain without a litany of complaints makes you stronger. Even if you are not able to overcome your source of pain, you create resilience by refusing to let pain dominate your life.

Humiliation

It is best not to waste your energy on the fear of looking like a fool. Instead, laugh at your mistakes and roll with your vulnerabilities so that you do not build up levels of self-blame and resentment. You do not have to look like you are always on top of things. Occasionally, allow yourself to be vulnerable.

Failures

Look at failures as humbling experiences that provide you with keys to future successes. The knowledge and experience gained through failures help you make adjustments that will continually improve your life as you keep looking for chances to spot and correct your weaknesses.

Death

You need to make close friends even though you may dread the possibilities that they may have severe accidents or die. Don't push others away because you fear that you may lose them. Develop death awareness and use death of loved ones as reminders not to waste a moment of your unpredictable existence. Strive to become a better person and keep on trying to better the lives of others.

Learn To Master Your General Fears

If you are patient with your mind, you will begin to identify more with your mindful self than the automatic thoughts of your mindless, emotional self. In doing this, you will feel more confident because you discard needless self-judgment.

Keep your plans in action even when things are going sourly. Refuse to be paralyzed by negative thoughts and remember that failure is not falling down, but staying down. Focus on the best possible solutions during the worst of times. (Viscott,1996).

More important than dealing with your limitations is your ability to acknowledge the strengths you have demonstrated during your failed opportunities. In doing this, never brag about your achievements because braggadocio is based on feelings of insecurity. Simply acknowledge what you do well and create a plan to better yourself each day (Goleman, 2005).

Get as much information as possible about what you fear. Expose yourself to many fear scenarios in order to avoid feeling surprised or overwhelmed by the unknown. Work on a checklist of skills that are necessary to face fears. The checklist should be used until skills become automatic and second nature.

One of the best skills you can master in facing fear is deep breathing. It helps you avoid panic and gets you to a point where mental relaxation and focus can be maintained.

HORNEY'S ANXIETY THEORY, JUNG'S EXTROVERTS-INTROVERTS

Horney's Theory Of Basic Anxiety

Karen Horney reasoned that some children developed a condition termed "basic anxiety" toward authority figures due to perceived rejection related to lack of caregiver warmth and affection. During her research on basic anxiety, she discovered that some children disguised fear of rejection by becoming aggressive ("moving against others"), while others channeled their anxiety into compliance toward adults due to fear of abandonment ("moving toward others"). A third group chose to withdraw in order to avoid further hurt ("moving away from others").

During adulthood, those who had been aggressive as children developed hostile approaches to life based on such needs as (1) need to be admired due to fear of being a nobody; (2) need for achievement; (3) need for social recognition and; (4) need to control and/or get the better of others.

Those who adopted a compliant solution during adulthood had overpowering needs for affection and approval that led them to compromise their identities and place the needs of others above their own needs.

Withdrawn children, the third group, chose an indifferent solution for adult living in becoming cold, rigid and by isolating themselves as much as possible, and held back their emotions.

How You Can Gain Control of Basic Anxiety

1. Check, catch and change your thoughts and feelings to ensure they are not unrealistic, rigid, and unhelpful. Remember that your feelings are based on what you think, so ask yourself "How is what I am thinking helping me become less troubled about this issue?"

Not only does staying on top of intense thoughts keep you focused during stressful situations, it keeps your friends, relatives and associates from "walking on eggshells" as they wonder what kind of mood you will be in across situations.

2. Go Easy on Self-Judgments. If you accept yourself, you become less likely to worry about taking growth risks. Do not allow your achievements to go to your head, however, and do not take success too seriously. Self-esteem should not be based on your achievements, disappointments or personality traits.

3. Eliminate Low Frustration Tolerance. Low frustration tolerance gives you the attitude that you can skip out on something that is trying your patience. When you give up too quickly across a wide range of situations, however, your lost goals pile up and you may have to settle for a dull, unproductive life.

High frustration tolerance allows you to meet challenges in a problem-solving, straightforward manner. With such tolerance, the struggle to achieve a goal is just as important as the goal itself because struggling stretches your possibilities and uncovers strengths that you did not think you had.

4. Distract Yourself from Emotional Distress. Use activities that distract you from distress so that you can mull over stressful issues while engaging in the activities. As you read, watch a movie, hike, travel etc., you can almost feel the tension melt out of your body.

5. Find Someone Who Is Empathic. Being in contact with someone who understands what you are going through and communicates the understanding back to you brings tremendous emotional relief. Empathy is such a powerful tool that the late, great therapist, Carl Rogers, used it almost exclusively to apply positive regard to his clients (Goleman, 2005).

Jung's Extroverts-Ambiverts-Introverts and The Needs for Control and Affection

According to Carl Jung, most of us are ambiverts who try to strike a balance between inclusion and being alone. Generally, ambiverts like to mix situations that they control with a state of being structured by the rules of the group.

Extroverts have strong needs for inclusion because they are energized by being around others, take pleasure in group activities, and tend to work well in groups. Extroverts find little reward in private time and they may become anxious and bored in solitude. They may interrupt more, talk more, become overly helpful in front of an audience and hold the floor longer in order to increase their personal influence.

Introverts have low inclusion needs and pursue such activities as computer use, reading, journaling and fishing. They become overwhelmed if they are faced with a great deal of group stimulation. They need to take care not to drift into unwanted solitude because prolonged lack of inclusion is detrimental to health and can be fatal. Lonely, single, widowed, and divorced people die earlier and have much higher death rates for each cause of death.

Due to the hectic pace of life in the modern world, Americans have become conditioned to building and ending relationships quickly. As we continually come to expect most of our relationships to change, we may become increasingly introverted and rely more on ourselves and less on others. Since our social behavior is largely based on our beliefs about how long relationships will last, our needs for affection and inclusion may continue to decrease.

ANXIETY 8

Glasser's Growth Needs, Nurturing, Cognitive Distortions in Relationships

Glasser's Growth Needs

According to psychiatrist William Glasser (1998), humans can use existential anxiety to promote growth needs for empowerment, belongingness, freedom and fun. He also included physical health needs in the total picture of mental health.

1. Need for Empowerment. This need enables you to assertively meet your needs without imposing them on the needs of others.

2. Need to Belong. The need to belong is fulfilled through friendships, romantic love and social connections. In building this need, make sure that significant others know about your anxiety triggers so that you will not catch them off guard when you become fearful. Even when you are overthinking worries, remember to stay in touch with the concerns of others who may need you at times to be their "rock" when they are questing for nurture and support.

25

3. Need for Freedom. If relationships become too dependent or controlling, they interfere with the seeking of independence and creativity. High freedom-seeking partners can balance things out with their low freedom-seeking partners by "checking in" when they are out and about.

4. Need for Fun. When you are having fun with others, whatever concerns you may have retreat to the "back burners" of your mind. Laughter, pleasure, enjoyment and humor give you much needed relief from the pressures that surround you. When relationships start going south, fun is often the first casualty.

The Physical and Psychological Need for Good Health

In order to keep anxiety from interfering with your relationships, you need a healthy diet that is high in Omega 3 and low in carbohydrates. Exercise and good sleeping habits are powerful allies in fighting anxiety symptoms. It is unfair for significant others to support you through your anxiety attacks if you are not doing everything you can to empower yourself through self-care.

Meeting Growth Needs Through Nurturance of Relationships

1. In this age of rudeness, a good place to start nurturing your growth needs involves kindness toward others. Smile more as you enter stores and restaurants, help someone with directions, or let someone get ahead of you in heavy traffic. According to self-perception theory, kind acts will change how you think and feel about your social actions and lead you to increased connections with others.

2. Weigh the costs and benefits of your relationship worries. The benefits of relationship worry (preparing for worst-case scenarios, catching problems early) are usually outweighed by its costs (reassurance seeking, jealousy, insecurity, anger). Such worries may lead to arguments and worsen your relationship insecurities.

3. Learn to tolerate uncomfortable feelings about fear of rejection and practice constructive discomfort to replace your worries, false assumptions, and seeking of reassurance. Use rejection as a "fuel" to build a better life.

4. Accept relationships as they are, and measure your thoughts before you jump to conclusions. In reconsidering matters, describe someone's behavior without judging it with your interpretations of the person's motives.

5. Learn to live with uncertainty and realize that you are limited in how much you can know about a relationship's future well-being.

6. As you lessen your dependence on others, they may wonder why you are not calling on them more often and become more curiously attentive to you as a result. (Leahy, 2005).

Cognitive Distortions in Relationships

Examples of Cognitive Distortions in Relationships (Reivich & Shatte, 2002):

1. He is angry, therefore, he will leave me (mind reading)
2. His working late means that he is going to leave me (personalizing)
3. If this continues, we will wind up breaking up (fortune telling)
4. I cannot survive without him. (catastrophizing)
5. I'm a complete idiot and loser in this relationship. (labeling)
6. It seems we are always arguing, so we will break up very soon. (overgeneralizing)

ANXIETY 9

SOCIAL ANXIETY

The Nature of Social Anxiety

Social anxiety causes you to worry excessively about doing or saying something wrong, think that people are staring at you, fear that you will freeze up in public, wonder whether you will know what to say during conversations and/or fear imperfections in your appearance that make you less attractive than others.

Your social fears can lead you to become extremely sensitive about how you come across to others. You may worry endlessly about exposing your faults, become easily hurt when criticized, or "mind-read" about being judged in a negative manner. Symptoms like blushing, sweating, trembling, and voice cracking can appear.

Causes of Social Anxiety

Symptoms of social anxiety can be traced to fear of being socially shamed. Such fears lead you to think that you possess features that need to be hidden from others. Other causes of social anxiety involve enlarged fear centers (amygdalae), having highly critical parents, and humiliating experiences in childhood.

Treatment of Social Anxicty

1. You need to learn that others will usually accept your flaws as much as you accept theirs. When you give up your efforts to keep your anxiety symptoms invisible, they will decrease and become less disturbing.

2. Practice a lot in order to prepare for social events. Read up on news events in order to converse well with others. Stretch yourself by starting "small talk" with others.

3. Show up early to social events so that you can meet people in small groups as they arrive. Such an approach means that you will not have to face the whole group at once.

4. Speak clearly, stand with good posture, make eye contact, avoid crossing your arms in front of you, and collect your thoughts when responding to questions.

5. Accept the possibility that you will be anxious, worried, uncomfortable, unsure that things will work out, and unable to control what people think of you.

6. Eliminate cognitively distorted social predictions:

Mind Reading:	They may be thinking I am an idiot.
Fortune Telling:	They will be thinking I am an idiot.
Catastrophizing:	It will be awful if I commit a social mistake.
Overgeneralizing:	I always screw up when I meet people.
Perfectionist Thinking:	I will not make a perfect performance.
Personalizing:	People at the party will not like me.

Emotional Reasoning:	I feel like something bad is going to happen, so it probably will.
Unfair Comparisons:	I will not be as smooth as the more popular persons.
Labeling:	I will be a boring loser at the conference.

7. Reduce intense negative thoughts that promote shame and anxiety.

The more you compare yourself with others, the more your self-esteem will drop.

Comparisons rarely reflect truths because people often mask their true emotions.

Unfortunately, modern day comparisons have increased due to computerized social networking.

Focus on becoming a "survivor." Survivors see stress as part of any life, construe changes as challenges, create momentum by "acting as if" they have enough energy left to pursue goals, neutralize their negative thoughts by moving forward with unfinished tasks, and remain flexible (playful or serious, tough or gentle, laugh at personal mistakes) in their daily behavior.

Cancel out avoidance tendencies. Although avoidance of danger and disastrous social situations are adaptive, too much social avoidance leads to empty feelings because you end up missing social events and job opportunities that could significantly enhance your life.

Malfunctions occur when you convert the shame of avoidance into anger that may power you through stressful days but makes you a buzzkill to others. Moreover, you may self-medicate the shame of social avoidance with social substitutes like drugs, food, and video games.

You may end up self-mutilating (cutting, burning, picking, sticking, and so forth) to self-soothe, to sense that you are still alive or to escape self-blame and feelings of rejection. None of these coping strategies provide healthy solutions to social anxiety.

ANXIETY 10

OBSESSIVE-COMPULSIVE DISORDER (OCD)

Obsessions are false, anxiety-ridden beliefs that keep replaying unwanted feelings in your head. As you try "not" to think about an obsession, it plagues you more because your brain keeps replaying it in order to remind you not to think about it. Obsessions keep eating up mental energy until compulsive rituals are often developed as misguided attempts to reduce obsessions and bring internal peace.

Obsessions or compulsions take up more than an hour a day or cause clinically significant distress or impairment. These issues cannot be explained by the influence of psychoactive substances, other mental conditions or the existence of a medical disorder.

People with OCD typically have dysfunctional beliefs that may lead to avoidance of certain activities and limitations in social and occupational functioning. Comorbid disorders with OCD may include depression, generalized anxiety, panic disorder, bipolar disorder, tic disorder and disorders that feature lack of impulse control.

Steps to Conquering Obsessions

1. Think of obsessions as drawn-out versions of your anxious thoughts. The key to reducing obsessions is to attack your anxiety-producing

beliefs that undergird them. Anxiety fools you into attacking the topic of your obsession (contamination, doubt, arranging, hoarding, and so forth).

2. Compulsive rituals increase your obsessive-compulsive behavior because avoidance of obsessive topics is temporarily rewarded with tension relief. It is good practice to expose yourself to feared obsessions, then use response prevention to reduce your compulsive ritual (Rothbaum, 2006).

3. Obsessive thoughts are not something you should expect to control. Curing obsessions is much like curing a cold-you do not get mad at yourself for sneezing with a cold, so you should not fight obsessions.

4. Learn to let yourself worry. If you practice response prevention of your compulsions and let yourself be as anxious as possible for a while, the obsessions will decrease because you learn that nothing bad ever comes from them.

5. Habituate (make an obsession seem routine and boring) by exposing yourself to your obsession as often as possible. Increase control of your obsession by decreasing its allotted time each day. This sense of control helps build your confidence and weakens the importance of obsessions. (Rothbaum, 2006).

Some Topics in Obsessive-Compulsive Disorder

1. Contamination. You become preoccupied with avoiding germs. Treatment of a contamination obsession involves touching (exposure to) feared objects, persons or places without washing (response prevention).

2. Doubt. You worry about something you may or may not have done and develop a compulsion which keeps you checking to see if doors and windows are locked, whether children are safe, and so forth. Expose yourself to uncertainty by gradually reducing your checks.

3. **Arranging and Ordering.** Lining up objects in a cupboard, for example, as noted in the film Sleeping with The Enemy, can make you feel more in control of your surrounding environment and life in general. Learn to leave your house or car slightly messy and let objects remain slightly off center.

4. **Hoarding.** You develop an emotional attachment to useless or worn out objects, often because you feel anxious over being isolated from others. Slowly teach yourself to discard useless items.

Obsessions in Other Anxiety Disorders

The obsessions in other anxiety disorders are not as severe as those of OCD and are less likely to produce compulsions. However, there are similarities between OCD and these disorders.

1. **Panic Disorder:** People with panic disorder may fear future panic attacks to the extent that the possibility of another panic attack dominates their content of thought.

2. **Phobias:** People with specific phobias may intensify their fears until they keep checking for evidence of their fears.

3. **Social Anxiety:** People with social phobia obsess about worst-case scenarios in social situations or something embarrassing or humiliating that happened earlier.

4. **Generalized Anxiety Disorder:** People with GAD overthink numerous worries and may become "worry warts."

DEPRESSION 1

COPING SKILLS RELATED TO THE SYMPTOMS OF DEPRESSION

Symptoms of Depression

1. Feeling down and out for no clear reason
2. Loss of interest in usual activities
3. Weight changes
4. Insomnia or hypersomnia
5. Psychomotor agitation (pacing, hand wringing, etc.)
6. Psychomotor retardation (very little movement)
7. Feeling guilty and worthless
8. Concentration problems
9. Feeling unable to perform ordinary activities
10. Thoughts of death and suicide
11. Possible grouchiness, hostility or impatience

Coping Skills

Cancel Out Bad Faith

Bad faith occurs when you connect most of the bad events in your life to bad genes, bad luck and bad people instead of your bad choices.

Bad faith can lead you to develop a self-pitying string of complaints and woes that drain your friends and associates. At some point, you may end up worsening your predicament with self-defeating choices like drugs, food, gambling, self-mutilation, etc.

In order to eliminate bad faith, allow your thinking brain to produce good habits and dominate the impulses of your emotional brain. During life's darkest hours, physical, mental, social and race/ethnic limitations amount to nothing compared to your determination to be at your very best. During severe tests that aim to break your spirit, you will become a much stronger person if you do not assume the quitter role.

Renew Your Meaning in Life

You renew your meaning in life by reframing stressful events as challenges and journaling your thoughts and feelings about unpleasant experiences. Writing things down helps you process images more deeply and develop fresh insights about your life. As you journal, you learn to distance yourself from bad events, develop new perspectives, and structure your days in a more efficient manner.

Enhance Your Sense of Belonging

You need to love, be loved and obtain recognition from significant others in order to feel as though you have established your place in this world. Children who failed to thrive in orphanages were much more apt to die from lack of loving care than from disease. Those who are growing up in the modern world are much more connected digitally than socially. Americans in general are becoming part of the "lonely crowd" that experiences alienation from the social world (Riesman, 2001).

Make Positive Connections with Associates and Strangers

In addition to renewing connections with family and friends, positive daily interactions with associates and strangers are vitally important to recovery from depression. When you connect with others through compassion and kindness, you strengthen your life as well as theirs. Children who connect to school and schoolmates see the world as a better place. Without connections, they may desperately seek social recognition to the point that they drift into choosing gang life or become school shooters.

Use Positive Self-Talk

Positive self-talk from your thinking brain gets you in motion with an extra burst of energy that keeps momentum flowing in your daily life. Stay with your thinking brain and mindfully observe how you relate to others, even when you are not at your best. Asking others questions about their lives, even if you are not feeling interested in anything, helps prevent social withdrawal.

When you take control of your life, you endeavor to find projects that capture your full attention. All you can do is all you can do. Do only what you can do without judging yourself by what you have gotten done when you were in a non-depressed state of mind. Positive self-talk and action turn down the volume of your negative thoughts.

When you can't seem to get going in the morning, tell yourself things like "My mind is trying to ruin my day. I will look like I care even though my mind is working against me." As you pursue positive self-talk, you take the initiative, change your withdrawal tendencies and become more courteous in social situations.

DEPRESSION 2

DEPRESSION AND IDENTITY

How Depression Plots to Steal Your Identity

Depression plots to steal your identity (your sense of self) by defacing your talents, character and other important aspects of personality that contribute to your sense of who you are. Depression brings up your losses, heartbreaks and rejections and saps your energy by interfering with your interests, concentration, plans you have made and hopes you have treasured (O'Hanlon, B., 2014).

Results of A Confused Identity

1. If you fail to trust yourself because you are not sure of your identity, you may fear that others will avoid you because you have become a nobody.

2. As much as you want to know who you are, you may become a social chameleon who changes characteristics, depending on your associates. Your personal traits become more formed by others' opinions than by your personal choices.

3. You may become a superficial person who feels empty and bored when asked questions about what you value in life. Since you have no

real identity, you may get frustrated when you are asked to answer a question about yourself.

Counter-Attacking Depression

1. Let depression know that you have what it takes to better your life. Fight its' attacks with positive self-talk about how you have made it through tough times and that you have emotional and social support if faced with hardships again.

2. Remind yourself that you will continually have to adapt to depression because it is a recurring nuisance. Tell yourself that you are quite functional most of the time, you can adapt to depression's attacks, and that pain is part of any life. Even though the "happy you" and the "sad you" must alternate, tell yourself that you will grow much stronger as you battle depression.

3. Challenge helpless feelings and develop skills that help you establish a sense of control over your life. View each negative event as a learning experience and replace negative thoughts with positive thoughts from a list of your strengths and enjoyed activities.

4. If possible, cut emotional vampires (toxic people) completely out of your life. If there is someone who continually brings you down, either remove that person from your life or create distance from the vampire whenever you can.

5. Don't try to make changes unless you are ready to change. Half-hearted efforts will erode your confidence and lead to depression-related slips and relapses. Take baby steps toward change.

6. Give yourself credit for good days and do not beat yourself up if you have an occasional slip into overthinking your woes. If you have become prone to self-medicate with alcohol or food, avoid drinking and/or buffet buddies.

7. **Do not overthink what people say to you because you may twist their words into slights that were never intended. Instead of wishing self-destructive impulses away, distract yourself with good memories and pleasant activities.**

How Structuring Your Day Provides Relief

A daily schedule keeps your depression at bay by distracting you from miserable thoughts. Plan your day in a manner that diminishes obsessing and worrying. Manage your time in order to curtail rushing to meet deadlines. Have a set place for your keys, wallet, and cell phone so you won't stress due to their loss. Prioritize your tasks and take on only one task at a time.

Journal your thoughts, feelings and behaviors and include time for rest, exercise, and self-care in your writings. Carry a schedule with you so you can consult it when you are too depressed to think in a proactive manner. Your schedule should include time for a social group or pet. If you have leaned too heavily on friends and family to take care of your daily needs, rebuild your responsibility for self-care and household chores.

As an example, you can start by getting out of bed and taking a shower. Then, you can move to the next activity on your list (for example, making beds, cleaning, doing laundry, etc.) and keep yourself in motion. If you use such structuring daily, your increased self-control will override weakly disciplined brain circuits.

Remember to use positive self-talk to tone down the intensity of negative thoughts. "I failed" becomes "I stumbled and will improve next time," "I can't" becomes "I can" or "I won't", and "I must be loved" becomes "I want to be loved, but my self-esteem does not depend on the opinions of others."

DEPRESSION 3

DEPRESSION AND COMMUNICATION

The Need To Connect To Others

Depression leads to poor communication when you become unable to see the cloud's silver lining in any given situation. When social withdrawal, inadequate coping skills, and fear of conflict are added to the depression mix, your chances for healthy communication skills can be completely crushed.

Reconnection will help blot out dark thoughts of suicide because the desire for reconnection enables you to think of the tragedy, shame and guilt you will impose on family, friends and/or pets who will be emotionally burdened by your death. If you can develop a larger purpose in life provided by such activities as child-care or membership in a support group, reconnection successes will help you "rise above the ashes" of depression.

Passive and Passive-Aggressive Communication When Depressed

When depressed, you may shift between passive and passive-aggressive communication. Passivity gives up piece after piece of your identity in order to please others. It may promote the false belief that "people-pleasing" will guarantee acceptance and love. You may have difficulty saying "no" without fear of social loss or "yes" without feeling resentment. At some point, your pent-up resentments may lead you to explode on those who have manipulated your emotions.

While aggressive communication openly disregards the rights of others, passive-aggressive communication masks your resentment and leads you to express aggression indirectly because you fear complications if you express open hostility. Passive-aggressive behavior involves sarcastic humor, withholding of praise when someone does a good job, muttering under your breath, saying "fine" or "whatever" a lot, spreading rumors, running late or sabotaging requests by agreeing to comply with them, then making up reasonable excuses for failure to complete your agreed-upon missions. (Paterson, 2000).

The Benefits of Assertive Communication

Assertive communication is the "cure" for aggressive, passive-aggressive and passive communication styles because it is clear, direct, has no hidden agenda, and takes in the perspective of the other person. Assertiveness is an effective way of learning how you and the other person feel about an issue. It allows you to say "no" when appropriate, reduces stress triggered by misunderstandings and builds your self-confidence as you learn to speak with clarity and confidence. Moreover, you learn to walk away from potentially bad situations.

If you practice assertive communication, you can gradually voice your feelings to others. Preparation allows you to go into situations with information about how another person may respond. If you know that a person tends to ignore or minimize the impact of your opinions, you can counteract such negative messages with improved "I" messages and proper eye contact. When you acknowledge the things you do well, you increase your ability to be heard by others (Paterson, 2000).

Examples of Assertive Beliefs Versus Irrational Beliefs

Assertive Belief: You have a right to put yourself first sometimes.

Irrational Belief: It is selfish to place your needs before those of others.

Assertive Belief: You have a right to change your mind.

Irrational Belief: You should always be consistent.

Assertive Belief: You have a right to interrupt a speaker when something is unclear to you.

Irrational Belief: You should never interrupt a speaker with questions

Assertive Belief: You have a right to be recognized for your achievements.

Irrational Belief: Don't feel proud when you are complimented.

The Need for Validation

When you express depressed feelings to significant others, it is important that listeners respond to both your words and non-verbal behavior (volume and tone of words, eye contact, and posture) in comprehending your complete experience with empathy. If you are shown that your depressed feelings are understood and accepted, your point of view is validated, even if significant others disagree with your opinion.

Validation also means that the listener probes to gain deeper meaning of your experience with "tell me how" and "tell me what" statements such as "tell me how it happened," "tell me what was the most hurtful part of the experience," and "tell me how you reacted to that opinion." Such probes help ensure that a depressed person's concerns are not being dismissed (invalidated) (O'Hanlon, 2014).

DEPRESSION 4

CHANGING THE EFFECTS OF HOPELESS DEPRESSION ON DECISION-MAKING

When you lose faith in yourself and the world around you, you may become hopelessly depressed. Prolonged hopelessness can neutralize your immune system, make you more apt to become physically ill, and push you toward suicide.

Aspects of Hopeless Depression

1. Doom. When you feel burdened by weakness and illness, a pervasive sense of doom may occur. Doomed feelings may also develop when you realize that you have wasted much of your life. The Columbine, Colorado, school shooters were enveloped in hopeless doom and even played a video game entitled "Doom" before they began their murderous rampage in 1999.

2. Disconnection From Others. You may feel like a hopeless outcast when you don't seem to fit in with others. You become depressed and socially anxious to a point in which you avoid interacting with others. Our materialistic, electronic culture is hugely responsible for disconnection because it is not user-friendly to socially active families, friends and associates. Excessive use of social networks, texting,

computers, video games, virtual reality and TV shows lead us into different disconnecting worlds.

3. Lack Of Inspiration. When you fail to find a model who can kindle a flame beneath you, you may grow hopeless due to lack of inspiration. As a result, you may wish to drop out of society due to despair. In order to be inspired, you need role models who live by higher values like kindness, mercy, empathy, honesty, multicultural respect and a sense of duty to all.

4. Feeling Limited in Opportunity. When you believe that your welfare is threatened by your perceived unimprovable station in life, you may think you have too many deficiencies to achieve any real success. Perceived deficiency often applies to both the disenfranchised and the handicapped. (Scioli & Biller, 2010).

Improve Your Decision Making During Depressed Days

1. During depressed days, easy decisions become tedious tasks because brain chemicals move more slowly. When making small decisions, it is better to gamble with making a bad choice than to remain stuck in a confused state. Never over-think a minor choice- simply make a choice and stick to it. Put off bigger decisions until a non-depressed tomorrow.

2. Remember to check, catch and change negative thoughts before they are blown out of proportion. If you have difficulty detaching yourself from over-thinking, turn your attention to tasks, skills and entertainments in your present environment.

3. Use effort-driven rewards that connect hands-on effort with mental effort. Journaling can be such an effort-driven reward because problems are processed more easily on paper and writing allows you to pour out emotions you would not ordinarily express. As you write, you access your analytical left brain, free up energy in your creative right brain, and better understand yourself, others and the world around you. (Lambert, 2008).

4. Reframing negative events by adding "even though" can hack away at depression. "Even though I feel despondent, I totally accept myself." "Even though I am having a mood swing, I can balance things out and move ahead." "Even though my partner deserted me, I have back-up quarterbacks."

5. Seek spiritual meaning that provides you with structure and purposeful direction. Spiritual meaning involves peace of mind and self-confidence that your chosen god will make everything alright for you. Spirituality also helps you understand the meaning of why things happen as they do.

6. Mindfully track your emotions as you would track each of your steps in a swamp as you try to avoid quicksand. Although you need to mindfully observe the drama of your negative thoughts, keep your distance from them and make no judgment calls. As you watch your thoughts roll by, turn your attention toward productive goals in the here and now.

7. You can never live a life without stressors, but tracking your thoughts and emotions helps you switch negative episodes to the back of your mind. When you accept things as they are, it does not mean that you like what you see. You are willing to admit that you carry emotional baggage but you do not allow negative emotions to gain control of your thinking processes (Hanson, 2018).

8. When you think about a situation, notice what your related feelings are, what the consequences of your actions will be and reflect on how to make wise decisions based on these considerations.

9. When filled with self-doubt and/or fear, remember to treat yourself kindly. After a hard day, focus on being grateful instead of beating yourself up by overthinking the day's bad moments. Do not get snippy or cop an attitude due to frustration.

DEPRESSION 5

DISCONNECTION THROUGH GUILT, SHAME AND LONELINESS

Keep Your Initiative Alive and Well

The eminent writer Erik Erikson asserted that young children needed initiative to master their environments if they were to avoid feelings of anxiety, guilt and doubt. According to Erikson, unresolved initiative lowered children's self-esteem needs and led them to either withdraw or vent their frustrations in an antisocial manner. If such scenarios were not corrected, maladaptive issues could lead to mental disorders.

As a depressed person, you need to be assertive, define yourself according to your perceived strengths and weaknesses and remain aware that your mind's random chatter can distort reality if you fail to stay mindful. Do not let your concern over how others feel about you downgrade your self-esteem. Similarly, refuse to place blame on yourself when you are not at fault and do not feel guilty about your trivial mistakes.

The Good and Bad Sides of Guilt

Guilt is often a healthy feeling that motivates you to stop behaviors that go against your values. It often leads you to apologize, change your ways, and reconnect with others. Just remember that guilty feelings need to point to a specific action you took, or failed to take, not to uncontrollable thoughts and feelings that flash through your mind.

Guilt is related to either lack of self-control or blown commitments to others. In terms of self-control, you may feel guilty about such acts as eating or drinking too much, not exercising, procrastinating or wasting money. Commitment violations may include cheating on your partner, not spending enough time with family and friends, ignoring certain work duties, and so forth (Reivich & Shatte, 2002)

When guilty, forgive yourself just as you might forgive a friend or associate who did you wrong. Demonstrate a true willingness to make peace with those who may have harmed you and be willing to make restitution when you have wronged someone. As an empathic, self-aware person, push the guilt button for a few minutes, then forgive yourself with heartfelt repentance and a strong resolve to change your behavior. If you mindlessly continue to dwell on things you regret, you will most likely sink into a bout of deep depression (O'Connor, 2010).

Shame

Shame is a close cousin of guilt. While beliefs that precede guilt focus on having committed a bad action, beliefs that lead to shame center around the label of being a bad person. Shame may lead you to disconnect from others and see yourself as a social outcast who is less than human. In such a state, you never feel quite comfortable due to inferiority feelings that remind you how you don't quite fit in.

Shame often develops when people witness your wrongful or embarrassing acts, making self-acceptance hard to come by as your mistakes sap your energy, keep you dwelling on your faults, and prevent you from moving on with your life. Social anxiety, substance abuse, eating disorders, killing rampages and a host of other personal and social problems ensue from such a disturbing sense of alienation (Briggs, 1999).

Shame can be useful in setting social values. Fathers who fail to pay child support are labeled "deadbeat dads," people who are arrested for miscellaneous crimes may be photographed and placed in newspapers, sex offenders are mandated to sign public registries, and politicians who use inappropriate terminology rarely win elections. In such cases, shame may be useful as a deterrent to continued criminal behavior.

Loneliness

Intense shame may lead you to experience deep loneliness. When you feel excluded, your brain senses a threat to survival and releases pain signals in the same manner in which it would if you were being threatened with real physical harm. Your immune system may become impaired if the stress hormones of loneliness never really die down. Inflammation leading to arthritis, diabetes and heart disease may set in. The increased mortality rates of loneliness sufferers compare to those of tobacco smokers.

In order to overcome this isolated state, you need to develop approach behaviors that allow you to gradually expose yourself to dreaded social situations. In preparing yourself for social occasions, work on improving your persona (public self) by making eye contact, greeting people with a smile, rehearsing common social interactions and learning what to say in a variety of social situations.

DEPRESSION 6

DISTORTED THOUGHTS THAT CAN LEAD TO DEPRESSION

Sensory Overload and Distortions

The human brain cannot handle all the information taken in by the senses. In order to deal with sensory overload, humans make assumptions without thinking through "whys" and "wherefores" of situations. These intuitions are often correct, but they can lead to distorted self-talk that may increase depressive thinking. Distortions and depression may involve a reciprocal process- distortions may cause depression and depression may cause distortions.

Examples of distortions that can deepen depression include "If I make one mistake, I will lose everything;" "I must never show my real emotions;" "If I am not compliant with their wishes, I will not be respected;" "I am nothing without a partner."

On the other hand, short-cuts that decrease depression could include: "I like challenges;" "I am respected by everybody;" "I am in total control of my life;" and "I will always be stronger after I learn from my failures."

Some Cognitive Distortions That Can Increase Depressive Thinking

1. All or Nothing Thinking. You see situations in "all good" or "all bad" extremes when most things in life involve shades of gray, or middle grounds. Instead of citing yourself as either a good or a bad person, you need to see yourself as a person who does a lot of good things, but also one who makes occasional poor decisions.

2. Overgeneralization. You generalize events into overall life patterns. If you fail to make a sale, you may generalize that you are going to be bad in business. If a man is rude to a woman, she may generalize that "all men are rude."

In extreme forms of overgeneralization, you put a label on yourself or others based on limited evidence. There is no reason to perceive a single failure as evidence that life is hopeless. You simply need to change the way you approach a negative event and not allow it to destroy your dreams.

3. Disqualifying the Positive. Instead of feeling good after being complimented, you may attribute compliments to people "who are just being nice." When praised, you may say it was undeserved and attribute the nice outcome to others. When rewarded, you say things like "The boss was in a great mood," "I was lucky to be there at the right time and place," or "The company was just keeping quotas for race, ethnicity and gender in mind."

This type of distortion continues to cloud your mind even when there is clear evidence that the distortion was misguided and wrong.

4. Jumping to Conclusions: Mind Reading and Fortune Telling. Although it is possible to have some idea about what others are thinking, mind reading can distort what you believe to be the thoughts of others. For example, when a person frowns or grimaces at you, (s)he may be reliving negative thoughts instead of thinking bad things about you.

Fortune telling involves negative predictions for your future career, health, and relationships. For example, "If I go on a diet, I will have the same experiences as Oprah Winfrey;" or "On-line dating will simply bring me more heartaches." Most of your intuitions can benefit from having additional data. When you eliminate jumping to conclusions, you become less impulsive and take more control of your emotional life.

5. Catastrophizing. When you think that things are worse than they really are, you make "mountains out of molehills." As Mick Jagger stated in a recent Rolling Stones song entitled "Doom and Gloom," there are many potential outcomes other than disasters predicted by worst-case scenarios.

"De-catastrophize" by challenging your "doom and gloom" self-statements. For example, "All humans are error-prone. I will not get kicked off the team for making two errors in a baseball game. I just need to concentrate a little more on fielding ground balls and I will do better in the future."

6. Personalizing and Externalizing. With personalizing, you instinctively blame yourself for problems without checking for facts. If a friend does not text you back immediately, you assume you have done something to make the person angry or disgusted with you. Such an assumption decreases your confidence and deepens your depression.

Externalizing blames others or situations for your plight when things go wrong. Although putting the blame on others or situations may reduce your self-doubt and increase your self-esteem, it may blind you to causes of problems that may be within your control. Furthermore, blaming others/situations can make you more prone to anger.

7. Should Statements. Should statements are based on beliefs about what you or others "should" do, "ought" to do, or "must" do. Albert Ellis coined the term "musturbation" to identify the unrealistic

demands that people place on themselves, others, and the world around them.

Should statements lead to guilt when you don't live up to impossible standards. Similarly, you may develop resentments when others do not live up to your expectations. It is best to use the word "prefer" and eliminate "should" statements. "Prefer" can also be used as a substitute word for "ought" and "must" when you address your actions as well as those of others.

DEPRESSION, DEPENDENCY AND CODEPENDENCY

Independent Relationships

A well-balanced relationship is not a smothering, "joined at the hip" ordeal. When you balance time together and me-time, you create both togetherness and independence because partners need to have clear identities apart from their relationships. Everyone needs personal time, and occasional space gives partners more topics to talk about. When you trust your partner, you feel more secure and your relationship serves to create a buffer between you and the difficulties in life. A foundation built on trust gives each partner positive energy to get through life's ups and downs (Neenan, 2009).

Dependency

In a dependent relationship, a type of parent-child relationship develops when the weaker partner expects 24/7 protection from the stronger partner and sees personal time as a depressing type of punishment. Too much dependency creates arguments, resentment and destroyed relationships. In order to prevent such a situation, the stronger partner needs to communicate that periodic absence does not indicate a lack of care or that the weaker partner is being punished. The weaker partner needs to understand that clinging and needy people are often dismissed.

If you are a dependent partner, you may become depressed, prone to being used and abused and you may get trapped in a situation in which you can neither speak up nor leave. On the other hand, if you are so dependent that you disallow your partner "me time," it is your partner's right to demand "a breath of fresh air." When both partners enjoy personal time, there is a better chance that the relationship will flourish (McQuaid & Carmona, 2004).

Personal Boundaries and Depression

When you wrap strong boundaries around your personal space, you demand respect, protect yourself from being manipulated, and avoid those who do not have your best interests at heart. Weak boundaries make you vulnerable to being taken for granted and possibly damaged by others. As a depressed person, you may loosen your boundaries and decide to care more about others' feelings than your own. In this state of mind, you may blame yourself for things that are not your fault and/or feel guilty about feeling needy.

On the other hand, your depression may lead you to rigid boundaries. Instead of having the loose boundary problem of not protecting your own needs, you may become too distant, cold, isolated and lonely to talk openly with others (Lancer, 2014).

Codependency

In a codependent relationship, each partner leans on the other to a point where their boundaries become fused together and their identities become distorted. Each person loses track of what it takes to be committed to a healthy identity and neither can feel truly whole because personal needs are sacrificed for those of the partner. The partners are in a bind because neither can escape empty feelings when not depended upon to fill the role of victim or enabler.

Expected Returns in a Codependent Relationship

Victims dwell on past injustices to the point that they cannot move on with their lives. They may seek relief with various forms of addiction, blame others for their shameful habits and sacrifice their boundaries and identities in hopes that they will gain support that they think they need from enablers.

The "victimized" partner expects an enabler to be a personal savior and "fix" personal problems (for example, drug, food, sex, gambling, and other types of addictions). Victims need to reframe their self-pitying attitudes and view past events as learning experiences from which good things may come. They need to take ownership of problems instead of blaming others for their vacant lives.

Similarly, enablers' neediness for love and affection drives them to take the blame for victims' problems. Enablers try to fix lives in order to feel more valued and respected. They do not try to save victims because they truly care about a victim's problems, but because they expect love and appreciation in return.

If enablers really wanted to save victims, they would encourage them to fix their own problems. Enablers have spent their lives feeling valued and loved only when they proved to be of some use to someone. As a result, letting go of fixing is very scary to them (Lancer, 2014).

Protecting Boundaries: Final Thoughts

Honoring who you are and what you will accept protects you and others in your relationships. When you have loving, strong boundaries, you retain healthy self-esteem, a sense of safety and resilience that empower you to fight depression. You understand that partners need to support each other in their respective searches for growth and development, and that they cannot accommodate each other all the time (Lancer, 2015).

DEPRESSION 8

BEHAVIOR CHANGE AND DEPRESSED MOOD

The Reciprocal Relationship Between Behaviors and Emotions

It has been argued that a person must be in the right mood if behavior is to be changed. According to this point of view, you need to feel love or lust for someone before you can make love to the person, or you need to feel anger toward someone before you use physical force against the person.

As self-perception theory has indicated, the reverse is often true. For example, the behavior of giving a small gift to charity can make you change your self-perception from an overly frugal person to a kinder, more compassionate being. In the world of theater, you may fall in love with someone because you perform the behaviors of "acting as if" you are in love with that person. Similarly, in dominance and submissive relationships, partners may feel love as they volunteer to produce and submit to acts of torture "as if" they are lustful forms of bonding leading to love, not anger.

Change Behavior, Then Your Moods Will Start to Change

The fastest way to change an unpleasant emotion is to change the behaviors that are attached to it. Choosing healthy plans, goals and activities, regardless of the mood you are in, is better than waiting for your mood to change before you make a move in the right direction. If you are lost on a highway, you will take action to get to your destination instead of waiting to get in a better mood before you develop a plan.

In developing a behavior change plan, ask yourself:

"What do I really want?"

"What am I doing to get what I want?"

"How are my plans, goals and activities helping me get what I want?" (Glasser, 1965).

Overcoming Bad Faith Rationalizations

The bad faith section is Depression 1 can be construed as a form of rationalization that relates especially well to feelings of depression. A depressed mood may lead you to blame your depression, genes, parents, teachers, bosses, friends and lovers for your miserable state when all you really need to do is admit to yourself that, regardless of how you feel, you almost always have the ability to decide what to do with your time.

When you rationalize your maladaptive behavior, you miss out on challenges and chances to find answers to unanswered questions. You never really achieve closure with items on your bucket list because you pass up chances to improve your life. As time passes, you may feel considerable guilt until you come face-to-face with your need to be a contributing member of society. Rationalization will be discussed further in Stress 7 which deals with defense mechanisms.

Incentives And Moods

You can act independently of your moods if you have sufficient incentives. For example, if you are reluctant to go to a ceremony, you will probably attend if someone offers you $500.

You can simply feel what you feel and still keep pursuing your goals. When you go against a bad mood and stretch your comfort zone by "acting as if" you are motivated to pursue a goal, your motivation to move toward a goal is increased (Greitens, 2015)

Avoidance Behaviors Related to Depression

Avoidance behaviors, discussed under Social Anxiety in Anxiety 9, can be very useful in difficult and dangerous situations, but attempts to avoid bad feelings (drug abuse, overeating, for example) are unhealthy, and can trigger other problems. There are many ways to soothe depressive feelings without using drugs, food, gambling, self-mutilation or sex. Hiking or strolling, gardening, fishing, drinking a cup of tea, and listening to smooth sounds of waterfalls, rain, ocean waves, etc. provide excellent examples of pleasant ways to treat yourself well (Glasser, 1976).

Overthinking

If you choose to face depression, you live in the present more than the past or future and feel spiritually connected to some higher power. When filled with self-doubt or fear, you learn to treat yourself kindly. After a hard day, you focus on being grateful instead of beating yourself up with bad memories.

Although thinking deeply about problems can help you figure out some practical matters, you need to spend less time dwelling on your mistakes and more time attending to something productive. If you stay productive, you are more likely to remain on top of what you are sensing, thinking and feeling in the present moment.

Overthinking complicates your life because brooding and stewing over matters drive you toward self-criticism and pessimism. As you overthink, you become lost in your own head, lose touch with things around you and fail to fully perceive what people are saying to you.

Even when you have little control over your environment, you can have a great deal of perceived personal control that helps you power through bouts of depression. By choosing to perceive control over a situation, you decrease depression as, for example, you determine how you will react to a dreaded medical report or unfavorable lover's decision (Reivich & Shatte, 2002).

DEPRESSION AND BIPOLAR DISORDER

Agitated Vs. Typical Depression in Bipolar Disorder

The depressive aspect of bipolar disorder often presents as an emotionally agitated, irritable, anxious, restless, unsettled mood state due to a mixture of depression, anxiety and mania.

Symptoms of agitation include pacing back and forth, fidgeting, hand wringing, leg shaking, rocking, picking and pressured speech caused by racing thoughts.

Agitation can run the gamut from mild to dangerous- anger, violence, self-mutilation and suicide attempts may result from such a state. When psychotic features are attached to this condition, suicidal and homicidal issues become more pronounced.

Examples of Typical and Agitated Depression

1. I cry unpredictably for no clear reason
2. I often dislike the way I look
3. I sometimes feel irritable and angry without really knowing why
4. Sometimes I pace and fidget a great deal
5. It is hard to wake up and get going most mornings

6. Regardless of my sleep time, I never wake up feeling refreshed
7. Sometimes I speak more slowly than usual
8. Sometimes I speak more rapidly than usual
9. My interests and pleasures seem to be fading
10. At times, I feel hopeless and worthless
11. I either overindulge or starve myself
12. I experience thoughts of death and suicide
13. I have experienced weight changes

Descriptive Features of Manic and Hypomanic Aspects of Bipolar Disorder

Mania is an excitable rise in mood that involves racing thoughts, restlessness, pressured speech, increased energy, a surge in confidence, desire for constant excitement, decreased need for sleep and involvement in many unfinished projects due to poor concentration. Hypomania is a less intense version of mania and it can actually be an energizing, creative force if treated properly.

During manic states, you develop sensory overload (overstimulation) to the point that sounds may seem to get louder, colors may appear to be brighter, you become more impulsive and you may spend, drive, gamble and/or have sex recklessly. The chance exists that you may go several nights without sleeping. The feel-good, impulsive rush of mania can turn on a dime, however, and you may quickly develop angry mania with destructive and/or self-destructive thoughts.

Tips for Dealing with Mania / Hypomania

Catch sensory over-stimulation before it gets out of hand by staying on a structured schedule and reducing your activities. Push yourself to stay with a project until it is finished. Read, watch TV shows, stay as relaxed as possible, and avoid loud gatherings of people. When talking to others, do not interrupt.

Write down each new project, give it a high or low priority number and complete the highest numbered tasks one at a time. Exercise in order to "reset the focus button" in your mind. When making a decision, use a 24-hour waiting period to think about risky projects that you would not ordinarily undertake. Remember to control caffeine, nicotine and stimulant drugs when you are in an overstimulated state.

Examples of Mania

1. I talk more than usual.
2. I talk faster than usual.
3. I get more impatient and irritable than usual.
4. I become more stubborn, bossy and determined to get my way.
5. I have sleep problems due to racing thoughts, anxiety and nightmares.
6. I argue more with others.
7. I am touchy and easily annoyed when people question my excitement.
8. I may become spiteful and revengeful.
9. When I am not too manic, I am very creative.
10. I may get too happy and too sad during the same day.
11. I get more energetic and excited late in the day.
12. I am hard to calm down when emotional.
13. I can get really anxious, panicky, nervous and suspicious.

Mania or Attention Deficit Hyperactivity Disorder

Mania is similar to attention deficit hyperactivity disorder- both disorders feature overactive behavior, lack of attention, high energy, poor impulse control, talkativeness, irritability and moodiness.

Unlike ADHDs, however, people with mania often have trouble getting going in the morning, are prone to depression, and may take a long time to calm down when angered. Those with manic features may experience decreased need for sleep and possibly have issues with nightmares, paranoia, hallucinations and delusions.

HOW MINDFUL EATING DECREASES DEPRESSION

Mindless (Emotional) Eating

Emotional eating involves a desperate search for comfort coming from high-carb foods. There is no physical hunger with this mindless eating, only a psychologically-based hunger that features impulsive, trance-like, autopilot eating, along with possible drinking of empty calorie beverages. Eating comfort foods that nourish serotonin receptors in your brain may calm you down and make you feel cared for, but the practice can lead to unintended psychological and medical disasters like depression, obesity, heart attacks, diabetes, and many other harmful conditions.

Emotional eating may occur out of convenience. When you are depressed and lack energy, fast food drive-throughs and the nearby food items in your kitchen may be the most appealing choices. If you are a depressed person who finds it difficult to function without strict structure and routine, you may get hooked on a self-destructive pattern such as eating pastries for breakfast, burgers and fries for lunch and fried pork chops for dinner.

Then again, you may experience decreased appetite when depressed and end up missing meals because you get stuck in an inert state that reduces motivation and energy to eat. Your depression may worsen and you become irritable and hypersensitive from not eating sufficient amounts of food.

Emotional Eating Versus Binge Eating Disorder

The key difference between emotional and binge eating is the amount of food ingested.

Binge eating disorder is a form of mental illness that involves an average of one compulsive eating episode a week for at least a three-month period. The person with binge eating disorder may eat fast, conceal the amount eaten out of shame and guilt, and feel disgusted with self after a binge episode.

Mindful Eating

Mindful eating involves monitoring what and how much you eat as you react to physical hunger. When you are mindful, you pay attention to everything in your present environment and focus on only one thing at a time. When emotional hunger strikes, you limit your eating by noticing each bite you take. Mindful eating helps prevent depression, hair loss, tooth and gum erosion, heart problems, obesity and amputations (Albers, 2003).

When mindful, you do not fight the reality that you have an eating problem and you do not dwell on depressive themes of past hurts and injustices. Accepting reality decreases the intensity of negative thoughts that produce splurging or bingeing. As you accept reality, you become more able to power your way through overeating triggers with a daily calendar filled with activities.

Automatic Thoughts That Trick You into Splurging (With Solutions)

1. "It is Christmas and I can eat what I want." Solution: "A treat will not help me stay healthy. I can celebrate with something other than comfort food."

2. "I have had a rough day. I will feel better after I have an Oreo Blizzard" Solution: "I might feel better while splurging, but I will feel worse afterward."

3. "I ate the fajita, so I might as well have taco salad." Solution: "Yes, I ate the fajita, but I can get right back on track now."

4. "I'll eat what I want now and start eating healthy tomorrow." Solution: "If I distract myself and wait, the urge will probably pass and I can stay on my plan."

5. "If I were a stronger person, I could resist fried chicken and biscuits." Solution: It's not about strength, but practice." I simply need to keep a food log and be responsible for stomach hunger eating only."

6. "I'll never be able to keep weight off, so I might as well enjoy myself." Solution: Losing weight is difficult, but I am developing the necessary skills that are needed to limprove my health."

Tips That Reduce Emotional Eating

1. Reframe negative experiences as learning experiences. Replace negative thoughts with more positive thoughts from a list of your strong points and enjoyable activities.

2. Remove toxic people from your life. Once you accept the fact that you cannot change a toxic person, you save yourself time, energy, and depressed thoughts. If there is someone who constantly brings you down, remove that person from your life or create distance from the person whenever you can.

3. Avoid obsessing about what people say. Rumination may lead you to twist another person's words into false conclusions.

4. Eat three meals a day to secure protein. Plan protein or fiber snacks between meals to help fend off hunger and reduce the size of meal portions. Try to limit snacks to 300 calories or less.

5. Use a food log to monitor eating events. If you give in and eat something that has been prohibited, don't give up. Pick up where you left off and get right back on track. (Albers, 2003).

STRESS 1

AN INTRODUCTION TO STRESS

Stress and Primary Appraisal

Stress involves a tense feeling caused by unpleasant situations or issues related to overthinking negative events and being disorganized. Stress makes the immune system less able to respond effectively to infections, heart and lung disease, cancer and cirrhosis. Those who are at greatest risk for stress-related disease become too intense when dealing with financial issues.

Stress begins when your primary appraisal of (first look at) a stressor (unwanted event) tells you that the event may be overwhelming. If possible, make a challenge primary appraisal with stressors in order to produce eustress (healthy stress). Threatening primary appraisals, on the other hand, often produce bad stress (distress).

Secondary Appraisal: Problem-Focused Coping and Emotion-Focused Coping

In terms of coping with stress (secondary appraisal), problem-focused coping attempts to directly confront controllable stressors (for example, a school, work, or marital problem) by gaining information, planning, goal setting, acquiring new skills, seeking social support, resolving conflicts, and so forth. Emotion-focused coping, on the other hand, handles out-of-control situations by seeking distractions, gaining social support, and defense mechanisms. Events like bereavement (losing a loved one) require emotion-focused coping to work through loss and find eventual comfort.

Types of Stressful Experiences

1. **Daily Hassles (micro-stressors).** Everyday stressors like driving in heavy traffic, car problems, waiting in lines, work/time pressures and troublesome neighbors are daily hassles that produce psychosomatic symptoms in which your mind's reactions have negative impacts on your body.

2. **Negative Life Events-** Death of a loved one, job loss, and moving to a new residence or job location are some events that produce psychosomatic symptoms. Generally speaking, daily hassles are more stressful than negative life events.

3. **Frustration-** Frustration is the feeling you get when you fail to reach your goals. Low frustration tolerance may prompt you to think things like "I can't stand it" or "It's awful," while high frustration tolerance allows you to face issues like failures, losses, accidents, job discrimination, loneliness, isolation and hurtful interpersonal relationships without feeling extreme amounts of stress.

4. **Burnout-** When you are physically, mentally and emotionally exhausted, you may become cynical and emotionally numb to the point that you are distant with others and probably experience burnout.

5. **Conflict occurs when you are forced to choose between alternatives.**

Approach-approach conflicts involve choosing between two desirable alternatives. Some options are easy to solve (like choosing between pizza options), but forced choices between two desirable options (partners, for example) could cause you to lose an option that could possibly be your best choice.

Approach-Avoidance Conflicts involve choosing events in which there are possible good and bad consequences. For example, "Do I marry someone that my parents hate?" "Do I ask out The Incredible Hulk's attractive daughter and risk mutilation of limb and body?"

Avoidance-Avoidance Conflicts are often the most difficult to solve because you have to choose between two undesirable situations. Examples: "Do I get an abortion or have an unwanted child?" "Do I jump from the sixth floor into a net held by volunteer firemen or inhale smoke?"

Buffering Against Stress: Optimism And Practice

1. Optimists look on the sunny side of life. They have stronger immune systems than pessimists, who look on the dark side. Optimists live longer than pessimists because they think they can turn stumbling blocks into stepping stones.

According to Segerstrom (2006), pessimists can learn to be more optimistic. In the process, pessimists would experience less depression, fewer adverse physical symptoms, develop better coping strategies, and experience greater life satisfaction.

2. Practice. When you practice good choices until they become second nature, your brain begins to reorient itself in a more positive direction. However, bad habits will not go away for good unless you continually practice keeping them away.

When you have a bad day, you may wrongfully assume that you have wasted a lot of effort in practicing good decision-making but, in fact, the practice has improved your brain connections between your existing brain cells and new ones you have created by practicing healthy behaviors.

STRESS 2

REFRAMING STRESS-PRODUCING ATTITUDES

Changing Your Attitudes

You assign meaning to situations and thoughts through cognitive frames (stories you tell yourself). If you want to change the way you have been experiencing the world, reframe distorted stories that are based on your negative thoughts about yourself, your environment, and your future. Distorted stories can have a devastating effect on your attitude toward life events.

Self-Destructive Attitudes

1. Disconnection Attitude. You disconnect by losing awareness of the needs of others and fail to use compassion and kindness in your relationships. Your senses of adventure and humor are often cast aside and you may invalidate others by dismissing their ideas and feelings. You need to take an emotionally intelligent look at your personal growth and expend more time looking on the sunny side of life. Review the introductory part of this book devoted to emotional intelligence.

2. Catastrophe Attitude. This "I can't stand it anymore" attitude frustrates you to the point that you may give up easily and allow

71

problems to pile up. As you feel increasingly overwhelmed, your thoughts may dart around until you end up in a state of total confusion. At such a point, you may either shut down your emotions or run away from your problems.

A catastrophically-based attitude can lead you to create a "glass ceiling" that keeps you in your comfort zones and discourages you from taking growth-producing risks. You need to practice constructive discomfort and prove to yourself that you can make frustrating events less intense and smash your glass ceiling (Preston, 2008).

3. Worry Wart Attitude. This "what if that happens" attitude induces you to fret about losing control of your life when you feel completely overwhelmed. Distract yourself from worries by using positive self-talk like "what else can I enjoy right now?" Adding the word "else" implies that there is already something good going on and triggers a less worrisome mood (Leahy, 2005).

4. Stubborn, False-Pride Attitude. Such an attitude leads you to hold grudges and think that you have just cause to punish someone. Grudges end up hurting you more than the people you resent because they eat up energy that could be used to build a better life. Forgiveness releases the hurt from your past and the poison of your grudges.

Forgiving someone does not mean you will forget injustices or that you have to hang out with the person who has hurt your feelings. Forgiveness simply frees up psychic energy that can be used to attain your life goals.

5. Victim Attitude. This "Why me, Lord?" attitude keeps your thoughts mired up in past injustices. Since pain is part of any life, change your self-pity attitude by viewing painful events as learning experiences from which good things may come. If you become more flexible, you avoid letting victim status hamper your chances for successful living (Neenan, 2009).

Attitudes for Dealing with Difficult People (Neenan, 2009)

1. Tolerate Constructive Criticism. Learn to take constructive comments in stride and blame your self-doubt, not others, for your bad moods. If your self-doubt is noticed by others, they may push your buttons in order to make you feel inadequate in some way. Define yourself without looking through the eyes of those who could possibly harm you with their bad intentions.

2. Avoid Guilt Feelings If You Do Not Listen to Complainers. Complainers are "emotional vampires" who will drain your emotional energy if you allow them to persist with whining. You should respond to a whining request with an automatic "no'. It is not your obligation to sort out someone's problems- listen for a short while, then excuse yourself. Do not get caught in the thinking traps that a good person would listen or that you might offend someone by moving away from the situation.

3. You Are Not Responsible for Others' Behavior. If, for example, someone threatens suicide when you state that you are leaving, tell that person that you will feel sad if this happens, but you are leaving anyway because the death decision is not up to you. It is manipulative for a person to use a suicide threat in an attempt to control you by claiming that the act will be done out of deep feelings for you.

4. Try to Settle A Dispute Rather Than Remain Stuck. Stay calm and remember that some people may try to get back at you in some way after an unsettled argument. They may express grudges through passive-aggressive sulking, withholding affection or breaking promises that sabotage your requests with excusable errors of omission- "forgetting" to mail a letter, "losing" your keys, showing up late for appointments, and so forth. Review the book's section in Depression 3 on passive aggressive communication.

5. Don't Disturb Yourself If Someone Does Not Like You. Try to feel indifferent about it because it is beyond your control. You can only disturb yourself by thinking it is unfair to be hated. Notice and accept the hostility while moving forward with your life.

POSITIVE ADDICTIONS, THE "THREE CS," CHARACTER AND HOPE AS STRESS BUSTERS

Positive Addictions

Unlike negative addictions to alcohol, drugs, food, gambling, sex, and so forth, positive addictions are wholesome habits that do not push you to rely on things outside yourself in your efforts to combat stress. Positive addicts become dependent on activities that build inner strength and enable them to live as productive citizens.

As a positive addict, you choose a daily activity that leads to self-improvement and better control of your life. Some of the more popular positive addictions are reading, exercise, and meditation, along with creative expression through painting, sewing, gardening, and woodworking. Specific benefits of positive addictions include better mental health, energy boosts, less need for sleep, more self-confidence, and decreased irritability.

Instead of the negative addict's expended effort to escape life's struggles, positive addicts embrace challenges and gain extra vitality needed for achieving love, self-worth, pleasure, and meaning in life through meeting their psychological needs for power, belonging, freedom and fun (Glasser, 1976).

William Glasser, author of <u>Positive Addictions</u> (1976) stated that there were six requirements for a positive addiction:

1. It must be an enjoyable, non-competitive daily activity.
2. It can be performed without a lot of effort.
3. It can be enjoyed individually or with others.
4. You believe that it has some mental, physical or spiritual value.
5. You believe that it will continually improve you in some manner.
6. There is no self-criticism while the activity is being performed.

The Three Cs: Commitment, Control, And Challenge

The "Three Cs" promote positive addictions and enthusiastic, optimistic approaches to each day's dawning instead of viewing passing events in terms of boring drudgery. The "Cs" help you build a sense of mission that makes you glad to awaken with a fresh outlook each day (Brooks & Goldstein (2004).

Commitment leads you to focus on dignity, honesty, self-respect, love and personal growth as you become energized by family life, friends, recreation, social support and spirituality.

Control enables you to believe that you can cope with life's circumstances in most instances. The power of perceived control lies within your choices to take the necessary steps to make changes in yourself and your environment.

Challenge involves viewing changing life demands as chances to stretch your comfort zones and expand opportunities to pursue your dreams. It is much more effective to challenge an unhappy situation than to remain stuck in non-productive ways of living.

Reframe automatic negative thoughts that go against challenges: "I have too many anxiety attacks" becomes "I survive bouts with anxiety." "I am fearful" becomes "I am cautious." "I am shy" becomes "I am quiet." "I am out of control" becomes "I work hard to control my reactions" (Brooks & Goldstein, 2004). Review positive reframes noted in Anxiety 3.

Character: Having Moral Courage to Do What Is Right

Character is encouraged by positive addictions and the "three Cs." Character embodies self-control, respect, empathy, and kindness:

1. Self-control involves monitoring your thoughts and actions. When you think before acting, you become less prone to make decisions that could produce dangerous results. When you know that you can control your actions, your feeling of independence is boosted.

2. Respect prevents hatred, injustice and violence because it encourages you to treat others the way that you want to be treated. As you care about the rights and feelings of others, you end up earning greater self-respect.

3. Empathy entails noting and feeling others' concerns, as well as consoling them when they are feeling emotional pain. While sympathy involves feeling pity for others, empathy involves an accurate feeling of others' emotions.

4. Kindness is based on concern about the welfare of others. It induces you to think more about the needs of others and to stick up for those who have been troubled or bullied (Ginsburg, 2011).

The Power of Hope

There is a saying that "hope springs eternal." Hope is not wishful thinking, but self-talk that puts a lot of hard work behind productive goals. When you believe that the future will be better than the present, you will become more driven to succeed. When something bad happens, take one day at a time and remember that bad results will not last forever. When something good happens, credit yourself for your part in making it happen and allow yourself to be grateful for any kindness from others that made it happen (Scioli & Biller, 2010).

STRESS 4

COMMUNICATION BREAKDOWNS

There are a host of reasons why communication becomeS blocked (Neenan, 2009). Some of the main reasons for communication breakdowns are discussed below.

1. Stonewalling. With stonewalling, there is no willingness to exchange ideas on a topic. Neither party admits personal faults and communication is blocked by stonewalling aka the "silent treatment," and the "cold shoulder."

2. Put-Down Comparisons. "Why can't you be like your sister?" or "You are just like your deadbeat father" are examples of poisonous put-downs that spark defensive communication in others.

3. Dwelling on Past Issues. Mentioning one charge after another makes you focus more on attacking a person than problem-solving. You need to look at your own part in contributing to the lack of conflict resolution. If the other person is clearly at fault, forgiveness for your sake is usually the best way to move on from past hurts and grudges that erode relationships. Remember that holding a grudge is like taking poison and waiting for the other party to die.

4. Lying About Events. Knowing that someone is dishonest often leads you to disconnect from that person. Friends, neighbors and associates lose trust and back away from liars as they did when lying was discovered in The Boy Who Cried Wolf. Even when the boy was truthful, they refused to listen to him.

5. Inappropriate Anger. If you wish to persuade someone, speak softly with sincere, kind words. Anger is appropriate at times, but it should not be used in an explosive manner. Deal appropriately with your small issues before they build into resentment and grudges.

6. Dominance-Submission. The need to relate to others is so powerful that some people seek to end their isolation by dominating others in some form or fashion, while others seek relief from unwanted solitude by submitting themselves to another person or group.

7. Dependency. Being ignored and criticized during childhood can produce low self-esteem that leads to dependency. Instead of developing strong boundaries that help a person move on in life, the developing dependent dissolves boundaries to further the dream of being taken care of. The dependent often clings to others until (s)he loses respect and invites abuse because (s)he is far too willing to take blame in order to avoid abandonment by others (Paterson, 2000).

8. Aggression. The aggressive child can become overly competitive due to parental criticism or pushy parents who vicariously live out their dreams through the accomplishments of their children. Aggressive children need to do their best on their own terms instead of the relentless terms of their caretakers. As they grow up, they also need to develop compassion for others. (Brehm, 2002).

9. Narcissism. The narcissistic child models her/his parents' indifference and develops an aura of independence without need of others. As an adult, the narcissist is self-absorbed, lacks compassion for others and is preoccupied with power and success.

The grand illusion of personal power leads narcissists to seek and mistreat followers. They often lose their partners and children because family members of narcissists are often construed as part of the furniture instead of real people. The cures for narcissism are love, work and devotion to family life.

Brotherly or Sisterly Love: The Source of Good Communication

Mature, productive love is the best way to relate to others. First, you must love yourself, take responsible care of yourself, and know your strengths and weaknesses. Secondly, you must show love for your fellow humans, mainly by giving. As a giver, you express all the things that make you feel alive and transmit something beneficial to the lives of others.

Brotherly or sisterly love is the most basic kind of love. It involves the wish to better the lives of others through care and respect. Love of the helpless, the poor, and the stranger are the beginnings of brotherly love. Love only of self and family is not good enough because even animals love and care for their young (Fromm, 1956).

STRESS 5

SENSE SOOTHING AS A STRESS BUSTER

Soothing the Appropriate Senses

People often respond to stress according to the senses they value the most. Some people are most disturbed by unpleasant noises, others by troublesome sights, rough fabrics, unpleasant smells or tastes. Understanding which of your senses is most likely to cause distress can help you build stress resistance.

True pleasure often comes from enjoying the simple things in life as opposed to those that derive from adrenaline rushes. Self-soothing with life's smaller blessings helps you stay calm during crises, keeps mental crises from occurring, and brings on the pleasure of relaxation. The more you take care of yourself, the more you will be able to manage your emotions and handle difficult situations.

Touch

Touch is a pleasure that communicates comfort and caring if it is carried out in a non-threatening way. Without the minimum daily requirement of touch, you would not have thrived as a child. Suggestions for activating your sense of touch include giving yourself a hand or neck massage, wrapping yourself in a soft blanket, and cuddling with a pet sitting outside in the cool breeze.

One of the most pleasurable sensations your skin brings is warmth. You probably like sunshine on your shoulders, hot tubs, snuggling, a good hug, a hot water bottle on your neck, and sauna relaxation. Saunas are especially effective in reducing muscle tension and increasing endorphins which give you a relaxing sense of euphoria.

Sight

Your sense of sight can be soothed by looking at pictures, removing clutter, working on landscapes, and so forth. Since nature scenes are more calming than urban scenes, introducing plants, paintings, photographs of natural settings and aquariums into your home can increase your stress resistance. Look at anything that relaxes you or makes you smile- for example, a beautiful view, family photos, or dog pictures on the Internet.

Lack of natural lighting can produce winter blues known as seasonal affective disorder (SAD). Winter brings shorter days and more time indoors. People with SAD tend to sleep and eat more during the cold season and feel generally depressed from November through March. Spending more day time near windows and exercising outdoors can be effective in treating SAD.

Sound

Sounds can either provide pleasure (falling rain, smooth music, ocean waves, birds singing) or pain (jackhammers, blaring horns, revving engines). When exposed to noise pollution like construction work, arriving-departing planes, and television background noise for long periods, you may experience increased tension, irritability, and the development of a stress-related disorder.

The sounds of nature tend to be more pleasing than those of city noise. In minimizing noise pollution, use ear plugs to soothe your nerves and protect your hearing. Recordings of nature sounds (ocean waves, waterfalls and similar sounds) also help you relax.

Music can either calm and relax you or stimulate and arouse you. It lessens pain, speeds healing after surgery, lowers heart rate and blood pressure, and decreases anxiety and depression. The sound of another's voice (TV, radio, talking to a treasured friend or relative) can be quite soothing.

Smell

The smell of scented candles, a favorite cologne or perfume and aromas while bathing can be quite soothing. Smell is probably the most overlooked source of sensual pleasure. It is connected to the areas of your brain that generate emotional memories- this is why smells have such interesting effects on your moods and memory.

A smell like baked gingerbread that reminds you of your grandmother's home that you visited frequently as a child not only makes you remember what her house looked like, but it reminds you of the total feeling of being there. The smell transports you back to your childhood- back to the you that was visiting your grandmother.

Taste

You can derive more pleasure from eating if you cultivate variety, flavor, and texture with your food choices. Most of all, eat slowly and focus on the pleasure of eating. If you try to cancel out your fear of fatness with restrictive diets, eating can acquire so much importance that you may emotionally wolf down calories, regurgitate, and start all over again as wealthy Romans did during the decline of Rome.

You may diet in a vain effort to keep up with slim models even though you are not overweight by medical standards. Staying slightly overweight is healthier in the long run than yo-yo dieting. Low calorie diets often lead to frustration, fatigue, depression, low self-esteem and uncontrollable food cravings. What you need is moderation, combined with enjoyment of the taste of food and getting back in touch with your stomach hunger.

STRESS, ANXIETY, AND POST-TRAUMATIC STRESS DISORDER

What Is the Difference Between Stress and Anxiety?

The distinction between stress and anxiety is often blurred as seen in the case of PTSD, which was originally construed in the Diagnostic and Statistical Manual (DSM) as an anxiety disorder, but subsequently labeled a stress disorder. Generally, stress is seen as a short-lived reaction to a challenging or threatening event, while anxiety is considered to be a prolonged reaction that continues after a stressor has abated.

Although anxiety can be triggered by internal events like overthinking and worry, it is usually seen as a symptom of an environmental stressor. Those who argue for PTSD as an anxiety disorder state that people with this condition seek relief from sustained anxiety that occurs after facing stressors. They assert that sustained anxiety requires separate definition and treatment because it is not a simple by-product of stress.

PTSD

PTSD is an extended reaction to threatened or actual death, injuries or sexual attacks that cause intense fear and helplessness. Those who are predisposed to PTSD may possess fearful temperaments or hypersensitivity to hormones and chemicals when exposed to stressful events. Environmentally, these people may have been aversively conditioned by negative life experiences.

Physical symptoms of PTSD include flashbacks and nightmares, accompanied by over-arousal- feeling tense, easily startled, and having periods of sleeplessness. Emotional symptoms of PTSD may involve worry, feeling detached from people (numbness), depression, anger, and anhedonia.

Post-Traumatic Growth (PTG)

PTG occurs as a direct result of struggling with the aftermath of trauma. Features of PTG entail greater appreciation of life, warmer personal relationships, gradual acceptance of trauma events during bereavement, and a greater sense of personal strength.

PTG not only returns you to the way you were before tragedy struck, but allows you to thrive from the suffering due to life-changing shifts in relating to the world. In other words, thriving is a form of resilience that not only allows victims to "bounce back" from traumatic experiences, but also enables them to "bounce forward" and flourish.

PTSD victims who remain angry and unforgiving are likely to suffer most from PTSD, while those who accept traumatic events and give the events spiritual meaning often experience high PTG. Pre-and-post trauma social support, along with personality traits of optimism, extroversion and openness to experience, also correlate highly with PTG (Rendon, 2015).

Negative Beliefs That Hinder Recovery From PTSD

1. Belief that being anxious and depressed are signs of weakness.
2. Belief that it would be awful if you were not approved of by others.
3. Belief that others are always trying to spot your weaknesses.
4. Belief that you are socially awkward and not friendly enough.
5. Belief that you should let resentments pile up without expressing your anger.

Signs of Recovery from Negative Thinking

1. Less intense negative emotions
2. Increased compassion and kindness
3. More respect for your boundaries and the boundaries of others
4. Calm expression of feelings, taking one issue at a time
5. Better listening skills
6. Seeking win-win compromises
7. Taking breaks when anger gets too hot
8. Forgiving others in order to prevent resentment from blocking the pursuit of happiness

Special Case Of PTSD: Battered Women Who Kill

Many homeless American women and children are running from battering incidents by males. According to Lenore Walker (2017), the battering cycle of violence begins with tension build-up in a male that eventually leads to angry verbal abuse and possible pushing. The battering incident follows, usually succeeded by contrition in which the male repents. As the cycle continues, the male usually gains confidence that he can drop contrition and get through battering incidents without legal problems.

Women often fail to escape from battering incidents due to some of the following reasons: They may believe the culprit's contrite statements; have conditioned beliefs about the importance of the father in the home; lack the energy to escape due to depression; have deficient financial means for escape; and/or fear stalking and revenge against family members if they run to a shelter. Additionally, they may think that batterers will be released on bail if arrested and will get off with simple probation if convicted.

As noted in Farah Fawcett Majors' role in <u>The Burning Bed</u> and Jennifer Lopez's role in the film entitled <u>Enough</u>, battered women often dichotomize correct responding to homicidal and suicidal categories. Battered women need to demand respect and believe that they can escape their dilemmas without lethal action.

STRESS 7

USING DEFENSE MECHANISMS TO EMOTIONALLY COPE WITH STRESSORS

Defense mechanisms derive from subconscious thoughts that are designed to protect you from anxiety when other emotion-focused coping methods fail. If you use defenses too often, however, you may begin to lose contact with reality.

1. Denial helps you escape unpleasant events through initial refusal to believe bad news. Denial is not totally subconscious because you are somewhat aware of the information that you are resisting. Denial can be healthy when you use it to postpone some very trying situations, but it takes an unhealthy turn when you act in a manner that blinds you to such things as the faults of your children, the fact that your mate is cheating, and the possibility of contracting a sexually transmitted disease.

If you fail to read the results of an achievement or medical test, you may be in the procrastinating form of denial. Attempting to block out a painful time of your life or a root canal appointment brings on the forgetting form of denial. "Slips of the tongue" occur when a denied thought breaks through your subconscious and enters a conversation. For example, when you are forced to visit a disliked in-law in the hospital, you may slip up and say "I'm glad that you are sick."

2. Rationalization: Rationalization allows you to make excuses for inappropriate actions and/or appearing awkward. For example, "We would have won if the zebras had called the basketball game right." Another example would be a drunken minister crawling toward the church bus, insisting that he would have made it easily if someone had not stepped on his hand. A third example is the statement "if I quit smoking today, I may get hit by a cigarette truck tomorrow."

If you dress neatly to keep others from digging deeper into your life, you use neatness rationalization. If you want material things because you feel inferior, you use greediness rationalization. If you bring your mate flowers after elevator sex with a co-worker or knock on wood after saying "I've never been hurt," you use undoing rationalization. If you try to control situations by making wishes or thinking that you have to see three red cars to have a good day at work, you use magical thinking rationalization.

3. Displacement: Displacement directs frustration at targets that are less threatening than the target that initially caused frustration. A woman who hates her father may direct her ill feelings at all men. If she has not found true love, she may direct her need for love and comfort toward animals. Another example is the boy who takes his frustrations out on his toys.

A classic example of displacement would be a scenario in which a boss chews out a father, the father goes home and screams at his wife, the wife throws the kids' desserts into the garbage, the kids kick the dog, and the dog bites the cat. On a humorous note, the cat may be quite intelligent, sneak over to the boss's house and deposit a big hair ball on the boss's pillow because (s)he assumes that the boss started the whole mess.

4. Projection: Projection transfers your guilty feelings to someone else. Examples: A hypersexual mother focuses on her daughter's unacceptable sex drive; you lust for someone, then accuse the person of attempting to seduce you; a woman with hidden sexual feelings toward a girlfriend becomes overly concerned about the presence of lesbians in the community.

5. Regression: Regression allows you to return to a time in your life when things were more secure. You try to hide from stress through immature behaviors like bedwetting, nail biting, and temper tantrums, or you may giggle uncontrollably when you meet an attractive person. You may suck your thumb before a lethal injection or carry an old toy to work.

6. Reaction Formation: Reaction formation redirects an unwanted impulse into an opposite impulse. Examples: You become kind to a partner you despise (kill the partner with kindness) or spoil an unwanted thirtieth child with gifts; your secret sexual interest in a neighbor comes out as a strong dislike for the person.

7. Introjection: Introjection brings another's personality traits into your own personality in order to help you solve an emotional problem. Examples: A teenager imitates a musician to help him establish an identity; a widow dresses in her husband's clothes and smokes an occasional cigar to keep a sense of contact with her deceased husband.

8. Compensation: You try to make up for your subconscious fear of inadequacy. Examples: An unattractive girl develops a winning personality; a boy with a Cyclops-sized zit on his forehead becomes a dermatologist.

9. Sublimation: You turn earlier bad qualities into socially valued behaviors. Examples: a child who cuts up animals becomes a surgeon; a child who refuses to tell the truth becomes a lawyer. In terms of mental health, sublimation is a very constructive defense.

10. Identification: You try to build your self-esteem by living through other people's identities. Examples: You join a country club even though it means bankruptcy; you bask in the reflected glory of movie stars, rap stars, rock stars, and athletes.

11. Fantasy: You imagine events that will bring you out of your frustration. Example: A shy woman imagines riding with the Hell's Angels, her hair wafting in the desert wind. She also toys with the idea of riding Clydesdales with the Chippendales.

12. Intellectualization: You detach yourself from the strong emotional impact of a situation by acting as if the problem concerned other people. A loving son talks about his beloved mother's death as if he were a news anchor. A man about to receive a 12 AM lethal injection calmly states how he must repay his debt to society.

STRESS-BUSTING ATTENTION DEFICIT HYPERACTIVITY DISORDER

Overview of ADHD Stress

ADHD is a brain and behavior disorder in which under-stimulated brain chemicals and environmental conditioning produce distractibility, impulsivity, avoidance of tasks that require a great deal of attention, careless mistakes, losing tools, not listening well, forgetfulness, trouble getting organized, and failure to follow directions. All these liabilities lead to a barrage of stress-building corrections and punishments aimed at ADHD victims by authority figures and associates.

Additional stressors for ADHD victims include accusations of annoyance due to excessive talking and rambling speech, being poor listeners, and failure to play by game rules. Unless the brains of ADHD victims can somehow reach normal brain stimulation levels, ADHD symptoms will persist.

While parents, teachers and co-workers often complain about being stressed out by persons with ADHD, the under-stimulation, distractibility and forgetfulness symptoms of ADHD push victims into a chronic catch-up mode. When anxiety resulting from harassment by authority figures and peers is added to the mix, ADHD distractibility and forgetfulness become so stressful that victims may think of themselves as "All-American rejects."

Even super-intelligent people with ADHD become "stressed out" when they know they are as smart as anyone but fall behind others due to their inability to keep up with details. Since ADHD victims often see their lives spinning out of control, they may resort to extreme measures in order to exert some power over their environments.

Behavior Management of ADHD Symptoms

A highly structured life for ADHD adults and children builds security, self-esteem and focus on tasks. Since ADHD children cannot set their own structure, time out and loss of privileges work because stimulation is taken away for a set time period. Time-in imposes structure by having children perform constructive tasks during a punishable period of time.

It does not matter if a child appears unfazed by time out, time-in, or loss of privileges. These measures work due to increased structure and lack of stimulation if administered with calm, quiet voices that use ten words or less.

Calmness and conciseness are necessary because ADHD children will do anything to stir up rewarding stimulation. Additionally, it is necessary to be consistent with consequences because ADHD children will test limits on stimulation until the cows come home.

Reducing Stress in ADHD Sufferers by Increasing Their Self-Esteem

A good way to deal with the burdens presented to ADHD victims by genetic, biological and environmental factors is to increase their self-esteem.

1. The first step in building self-esteem for you, the ADHD sufferer, is to realize your inherited stress resistance that enables you to bounce back from adverse conditions, adapt to your struggles, and thrive from adversity in the long run. Aspects of stress resistance related to ADHD involve not comparing yourself to peers, reframing your deficiencies as gifts and finding ways to deal with situations that could diminish your confidence (Honos-Webb, 2005).

2. Work more on developing your strong points than on improving your deficiencies. Channel your distractibility and impulsivity into your creative talents. Recognize your excellent ability to read others and detect hypocrisy. Build on your curiosity about plants, trees, animals and preference for hands-on learning. Convert your hyperactivity into energy that makes you an exciting person who is fun to be around.

3. Structure your time so that you are not late to school or work. Punctuality and paying your debts on time make you feel reliable. Maintain your home environment so that you do not melt down due to clutter and smelly clothes. Make sure you minimize junk food and maximize a proper diet and sufficient sleep.

4. Utilize the benefits of exercise and stimulant drugs. Exercise keeps you better focused, builds mental endurance, reduces mental fatigue, and sustains alertness. When you need to push your "reset button" after exhausting your attention span, take a quick break, walk up and down stairs a few times, and/or do jumping jacks. You will then be ready to return to your "call of duty."

Stimulant drugs safely sharpen your focus, may be discontinued during week-ends and vacations, and help prevent self-medication with other drugs. Stimulants help you keep up with your study and work schedules, reduce the stress caused by lagging behind peers and help you maintain self-esteem. At times, they can be used for resistant depression that does not respond to traditional medication.

Stimulants should be taken with a "drug holiday" approach for week-ends and vacations, when possible, because tolerance can arrive quickly and needed levels of medication may be sought outside the law when pharmacy resources are exhausted.

STRESS 9

STRESS- BUSTING ADJUSTMENT DISORDERS WITH ACCEPTANCE AND SOCIAL SUPPORT

Adjustment Disorders

Adjustment disorders involve emotional or behavioral issues that lead to inappropriate reactions to stressors and/or significant decline in important aspects of daily functioning. Symptoms must appear within three months after the stressors commence and need to be attributed to an identifiable event (death of family member, break-up, family conflict, job loss, etc.) that disrupts a person's life. The diagnosis of Adjustment Disorder is quite common when there is an unclear clinical picture that requires sorting out over time.

Maladjustment in adjustment disorders is not the result of bereavement or an aggravated state of a pre-existing condition. The disorder does not meet the criteria for another mental disorder. Once stressors and their consequences have dissipated, adjustment issues disappear within a six months period. If issues last longer than six months, another diagnosis is made (PTSD, Mood Disorder, Anxiety Disorder, and so forth).

The six types of adjustment disorder involve depressed mood, anxiety, mixed anxiety and depressed mood, conduct disturbance, mixed disturbance of emotions and conduct, and unspecified (relationship problems, school or work problems, physical problems).

Psychotherapy of Adjustment Disorders Featuring Mindful Acceptance

In spite of your attempts to control stressful events, you are constantly threatened with things that are very hard to cope with. Accepting change as a chance for personal growth will decrease the negative impact that stressors have on your life. There are many life situations in which acceptance and emotion-focused coping must be used because the action steps of problem-focused coping are not possible.

Acceptance of negative events is better than resisting them with tension-building thoughts, emotions and complaints that drain your energy as you "make mountains out of mole hills." Instead of bombarding yourself with needless suffering, allow difficult thoughts and feelings to simmer and become consciously and subconsciously processed before you respond with action steps. Allowing negatives to simmer does not mean that you are giving in to them, but that you are measuring things out in order to conduct effective action.

Acceptance allows you to neutralize the "hurts" that keep popping up in your mind with mindful "what" and "how" questions, instead of victim-producing "Why me Lord?" self-statements that dwell on past injuries and worries. "What" and "How" questions focus on the present and push you to power on with small behavior changes each day. You mindfully ask yourself questions like "What do I need to do to regain control of my life?" and "How do I go about doing this?"

Social Support and Adjustment Disorders

Social support buffers you against stress and strengthens your immune system. With social support, your depressed moods decrease, you interact better with others, and your confidence level is raised. Studies have demonstrated how terminal breast cancer patients live longer when they attend support meetings. Even the presence of a service animal provides enough social support to boost your immunity.

When you receive social support, you learn conversational cues related to when to start talking and how to close conversations in a polite manner. When you choose your words wisely and speak pleasantly, you show respect and compassion for others. You learn to be kind and lift others up instead of putting them down.

Such support also provides you with non-verbal communication cues like eye contact, maintaining erect posture, smiling appropriately, standing the correct distance from others, talking in a loud enough voice, not crossing your arms during conversations and refraining from bragging when expressing your views.

When you share stories of struggle with members who have similar issues, your feeling of inclusion is reinforced. As you become accepted by others who have encountered similar pain, any feelings of shame that you may have fade and you feel more connected to group members.

When you are extremely stressed out by a shame-producing event, you may fear that you will either freeze up or do something stupid. At this point, you may withdraw and wish to become "socially invisible" instead of getting involved in situations that will improve your life. When you bottle up your emotions, you may ultimately select anger, your most powerful feeling, to blast your way out of a shame-producing situation. Social support can help you avoid this potentially self-destructive tendency. (Lancer, 2014).

Social skills gained from support help you work out unfinished business with family members, friends and associates because you process how to prevent conflicts that have troubled you in the past. You learn to become more empathic, helpful, and to stop being judgmental of yourself and others. You develop motivation to actively listen to other members, begin to feel more secure, get tension relief, and disclose more facts about yourself.

At some point, talk to social support group members about their spiritual lives. Spirituality adds a sense of meaning to your life by helping you figure out what is most important to you and enabling you to worry less about trivial issues. It can be a peak experience to have beliefs like those expounded in the Gospel of Thomas and the movie <u>Stigmata</u>: "The Kingdom of God is within you and all around you. It is not within buildings of wood or stone. Split a piece of wood and you will find me. Look beneath a rock and I am there."

STRESS, TEMPERAMENT, ATTACHMENT AND REACTIVE ATTACHMENT DISORDER

Temperament, Attachment and Stress

Temperament and attachment (bonding) are inborn needs that relate to one another. Temperament refers to the three inborn styles of relating to others: easy-flexible; slow to warm up (fearful); and difficult (feisty). If there is goodness of fit between baby and caregiver temperament, attachment security (bonding) comes easily. However, if there is a disconnection between baby-caregiver temperaments, the stressful state of attachment insecurity will result unless caregivers remain super-sensitive to the needs of infants.

Attachment issues will be more stressful for caregivers who are insensitive or inflexible. Nevertheless, such caregivers must go through temperament correction exercises for the sake of their children. When mothers learn more sensitive ways to parent and have solid emotional and social support to bolster their efforts, difficult babies are much more apt to become securely attached.

Four Aspects of Temperament (EASI)

1. Emotionality refers to how easily you become upset.

2. Activity refers to tempo (speed) and vigor. If you are high tempo, you walk briskly and prefer a faster pace of life than a low tempo person. If you are high vigor, you talk and laugh loudly, while a low vigor person talks and laughs softly.

3. Sociability either involves mild stimulation rewards like sharing an activity to make it more pleasant, gaining attention to prevent being ignored, or intense back and forth interaction that extroverted people enjoy.

4. Impulsivity entails acting in an uncontrolled, restless manner as opposed to a controlled, deliberate manner. Deliberative people plan well- in a marriage, at least one partner should be deliberative in order to minimize financial stress.

Four Attachment Styles

Humans carry patterns of mental and relationship functioning that were learned as children These patterns become frameworks for how their brains are wired to interact with others during adult life.

1. If you felt secure with your caregivers during childhood, you likely seek the company of others as an adult and think that connection can provide comfort during stressful times of life. More than likely, you experience low avoidance-low anxiety in relationships.

2. On the other hand, if you were treated with indifference by your caregivers, you may have experienced a great deal of stress and become high avoidance-low anxiety with relationships because you have learned to minimize the importance of intimacy. With this attachment style, you suppress your need for connection and regard yourself more positively than you do others.

3. If you have a pattern of high avoidance-high anxiety with adult relationships, you probably received a lot of criticism as a child and may often remember your more unpleasant human interactions.

4. If you received a lot of conditional love as a child, you may have become a high anxiety- low avoidance adult who craves relationships, but fears rejection. If so, you may become a dependent people pleaser.

Reactive Attachment Disorder (RAD)

Due to stressful issues with caregivers, a child may develop a pattern of disordered human interaction termed reactive attachment disorder. Typically, a RAD child's needs for comfort, affection and nurturing are suppressed to a point where the child loses the ability to develop loving, caring relationships with others. This stressful situation can permanently change a child's developing brain and hamper a child's ability to establish future relationships.

In the inhibited type of RAD, a child is withdrawn and fails to attach to either caregivers or peers. In the disinhibited type of RAD, the child exercises poor judgment, has inappropriate boundaries with others, and is overly friendly with strangers.

In either inhibited or disinhibited cases, RAD children do not value caregivers and often distrust them due to previous negative experiences. Since they received poor caregiving, they may see the world as a place where they must take what they can get by whatever means available in order to survive. They often have severe behavioral issues based on thinking that no one cared, so why should they care?

Reactive Attachment Disorder in Adulthood

Ambivalent RAD symptoms in adults include dependency, possessiveness, jealousy, frequent mood swings, constantly seeking to hear the words "I love you" from mates, feeling unlovable, being overly sensitive to blame and remaining in a state of constant preparation for short-lasting relationships. Avoidant adult RAD symptoms include compulsive self-reliance, lack of empathy, intense anger, avoidance of intimacy, and being critical of self and others.

Summary and Conclusions

The author's approach to correcting issues related to anxiety, depression and stress has infused curative factors grounded in resilience, willpower and emotional intelligence. Ten sections of material addressed to each of the three major topics of anxiety, depression and stress offer concrete growth opportunities to lay readers, students, instructors and professional therapists.

Anxiety

Anxiety has recently overtaken depression as "the common cold" of mental health disorders in the United States, thanks to multiple news alerts, war threats, the social media and constantly increasing digital demands that interfere with how we interact at home and work.

Anxiety begins to affect humans as soon as they can understand that people get sick, injured and die. Anxiety has been analyzed in an existential light in order to help readers convert anxiety into a growth force that spurs constructive action through the "four horsemen" of death awareness, responsibility that freedom brings, avoidance of isolation, and the pursuit of meaning in life.

Low self-esteem and irrational beliefs are steeped in anxiety. When overthinking is pushed to its limits, free-floating (generalized) anxiety, panic attacks and specific fears often raise their ugly heads. Karen Horney's basic anxiety theory and Carl Jung's introversion-extroversion considerations were added to the text in order to provide a developmental look at unproductive anxiety. William Glasser's growth needs for empowerment, belonging, freedom and fun were presented to deepen the reader's understanding of some of the existential aspects of anxiety.

While notes on nurturing relationships were added to enhance the reader's knowledge of human relations, analysis of cognitive distortions in relationships demonstrated how nurturing is thrown off-track by false beliefs.

Social anxiety has escalated in recent years, partly because of our digital world where video games and social media have disrupted confidence-building social experiences. Other contributing factors to social anxiety have been an increase in home schooling due to the rash of school shootings and dissatisfaction with the current educational system.

Obsessive-compulsive disorder is on the upswing as a manifestation of maladaptive anxiety patterns of coping with stressors in the modern world. Obsessions often spill over into other anxiety disorders and can lead to extreme withdrawal.

It appears that the maladaptive anxiety trend will continue to infest American society as our country becomes an increasingly digital and confusing place in which to live. Spiritual and social support groups may proliferate in order to curb the disturbing course of social, educational and occupational events. Governmental changes will help immensely if civic-minded people can someday replace politicians at the helms.

Depression

Although depression is no longer the "common cold" of mental disorders, it is closely associated with many mental and physical health diagnoses. In dealing with the symptoms of depression, you need positive self-talk, cancellation of bad faith and renewal of your meaning in life through new perspectives related to meaning, connecting with significant others/ associates, and by not judging yourself by what you can get done in a non-depressed state.

Depression attacks your identity in order to destroy your character and personality. Begin your counter-attack on depression's assaults by viewing negative messages as learning experiences that give you a chance to elaborate on how you became stronger each time you dealt with previous difficulties. Daily schedules help distract you from depressing ideas and lead you to monitor your behavior.

Since associates often avoid the "contagious nature" of bad moods, it behooves you to develop healthier communication skills. It is important to reconnect and develop assertive communication that keeps you away from passive, passive-aggressive and aggressive communication.

In order to prevent a nosedive into the doom and gloom of hopelessness, keep aiming at making good decisions by checking, catching, and changing negative thoughts before they are blown out of proportion. Effort-driven reward-seeking helps combat hopelessness by combining mental effort with hands-on effort. As pointed out by Erik Erikson, it is important to keep initiative alive and well in order to prevent a downward spiral into guilt and shame.

A close correlate of hopelessness is loneliness which may stem from the intense shame associated with social anxiety. Approach behaviors are needed to overcome both loneliness and hopelessness because both conditions pose a threat to your survival. In order to pull out of these self-destructive states, sort out the cognitive distortions that have sent you plummeting downward.

The plague of depression cannot be successfully escaped with either dependency or codependency because such adaptations negate your sense of self. It is highly important that you honor who you are with strong boundaries that strengthen your resilience, sense of safety and self-esteem.

There is a reciprocal causal relationship between behaviors and emotions. The fastest way to change a depressed state is to change behavior associated with it. It is best to keep struggling toward your goals regardless of how you feel. You need to focus on approach behaviors and choose to take action instead of remaining stuck in the self-paralyzing state of overthinking.

Bipolar disorder typically involves both typical and agitated depression. Agitation often involves restlessness and the need to keep moving around. In some cases, agitation can involve intense anger, violence, self-mutilation and suicide attempts.

The topic of mindful eating was covered due to the increased incidence of mindless (emotional) eating as a form of self-medication by depressed people. Mindless eating involves a desperate search for comfort that comes from eating high carbohydrate foods.

Mindful eating decreases depression when you accept the fact that you have an eating problem and need to reduce the intensity of your negative thoughts in order to distract yourself from eating urges. In pursuing comfort goals without food, exercise is very effective in reducing mental and physical health issues.

The rise in depression rates can be partially attributed to the lack of research in developing new medications. There is also a dire need for trained therapists to replace or supplement drug therapies. Since fewer than half of depressed people seek help because of feared stigmatization, military and political leaders, as well as celebrities like Dwayne "Rock" Johnson are seeking to erase the stigma of depression by "coming out" and talking about their personal woes (Jowit, 2018).

Stress

Stress is a universal phenomenon involved in many physical and psychological problems. Although it is usually construed in negative terms, it propels personal growth when stressors are perceived as challenges instead of threats. Since reactions to stress, instead of stress itself, are the factors that destroy physical and psychological health, reframing of stress-producing attitudes is essential to healthy stress resistance. Positive addictions to activities that build inner strength, along with commitment, perceived control, challenge, moral courage and hope, fortify reframes.

Stress-producing factors that block effective communication include stonewalling, put-down comparisons, dwelling on past issues in a non-forgiving manner, lying, inappropriate anger, dominance-submission, dependency, aggression and narcissism. Mature, productive love offers the best line of communication because it centers around the wish to better the lives of others through care and respect.

Self-soothing can be a tremendous boon to stress reduction if you focus on calming the senses that you value the most. Although the terms "stress" and "anxiety" are often used interchangeably, anxiety is usually seen as a reaction to an environmental stressor. Self-soothing can be especially helpful for those who suffer from some type of stress disorder. PTSD can be managed most effectively by the internalization of factors that promote post-traumatic growth.

Defense mechanisms can be used effectively as stop-gap measures when dealing with stressors, but excessive use of defenses can distort reality to a significant degree. Denial, rationalization, displacement, projection, regression, reaction formation, introjection, compensation, identification, fantasy and intellectualization may be effective at times, but sublimation appears to be the most productive long-term defense.

Although many people focus on the stress encountered by parents, teachers, and work associates who deal with attention-deficit hyperactivity disorder, those with the disorder often suffer stressful losses in self-esteem due to constant corrections, punishments and their inability to keep up in classroom or work assignments due to inadequate focus.

Adjustment disorders are stress disorders involving short-term disproportionate reactions to stressors. The diagnosis of adjustment disorder is used frequently when unclear clinical pictures need to be sorted out. In addition to short-term psychotherapy, social support helps those with adjustment concerns sort out unfinished business with family members, friends and associates.

A stressful state exists for children and caregivers alike when there is no goodness-of-fit between child and caregiver temperament. In order to prevent attachment insecurity, the caregiver must take an eagle-eyed approach to adjusting for temperamental differences. If re-calculations are not made, insecurity can carry over to approach-avoidance and ambivalent issues in adulthood.

Successful stress management has a lot to do with how one manages change. Alvin Toffler, author of <u>Future Shock</u> (1970) and <u>The Third Wave</u> (1980), was astonishingly correct in stating that "change is not merely necessary to life-it is life" (Toffler, 1970). He defined "future shock" as "the shattering stress and disorientation we induce in individuals by subjecting them to too much change in too short a time." (Toffler, 1970). Toffler went on to say that Americans would be better off if they dealt with change instead of trying to resist it:

To survive, to avert what we have termed "future shock," the individual must become infinitely more adaptable and capable than ever before. We must search out totally new ways to anchor ourselves, for all the old roots-religion, nation, community, family, or profession- are now shaking under the hurricane impact of the accelerative thrust... (Toffler, 1980).

If you can become flexible enough to accept change as challenging, not threatening, it will no longer "stress you out." Moreover, believing that your life will frequently change does not mean that you have no control of your life. You simply need to accept the fact that changes are going to come, and there will be times when there is nothing you can do to stop them (Toffler, 1980).

REFERENCES

Albers, S. (2003). Eating Mindfully. Oakland, CA: New Harbinger Publications.

Antony, M. & McCabe, R. (2004). 10 Simple Solutions to Panic. Oakland, CA : New Harbinger Publications, Inc.

Bannink, F. (2014). Post Traumatic Success. NY: W.W. Norton.

Bateman, C. (1995). Cycle Of Violence. N.Y.: Arcade Publishing.

Baumeister, R. & Tierney, J. (2011). Willpower. N.Y.: Penguin Press.

Bean, J. (1988). Effects of Individualized Reality Therapy On Recidivism Rates And Locus of Control Orientations Of Male Juvenile Offenders. Dissertation Abstracts International.

Blonna, R. (2010). Stress Less, Love More. Oakland, CA: New Harbinger Publications.

Bourne, E. (2010). The Anxiety and Phobia Workbook. Oakland, CA: New Harbinger Publications.

Brehm, B. (2002). Stress Management. Torrance, CA: Homestead Schools, Inc.

Briggs, R. (1999). Transforming Anxiety, Transcending Shame. Deerfield Beach, FL: Health Communications, Inc.

Brooks, R & Goldstein, S. (2004). The Power of Resilience. N.Y.: McGraw Hill.

Erikson, E. (1963). Childhood and Society. N.Y.: W.W. Norton.

Flach, F. (1997). Resilience. N.Y.: Hatherleigh Press.

Fromm, E. (1956). The Art of Loving. N>Y> Harper & Row.

Fromm, E. (1994). Escape from Freedom. N.Y.: Holt McDougall.

Ginsburg, K. (2010). Building Resilience in Children & Teens. Elk Grove Village, IL: American Academy of Pediatrics.

Glasser, W. (1965). Reality Therapy. N.Y.: Harper & Row

Glasser, W. (1976). Positive Addiction. N.Y.: Harper & Row.

Glasser, W. (1998). Choice Theory. N.Y.: Harper Collins.

Glasser, W. (2000). Counseling with Choice Theory. N.Y.: Harper Collins.

Goleman, D. (2005). Emotional Intelligence. N.Y.: Bantam Books.

Greitens, E. (2015). Resilience. N.Y. Houghton Mifflin Harcourt.

Hanson, R. (2018). Resilient. London: Ryder.

Honos-Webb, L. (2005). The Gift Of ADHD. Oakland, CA: New Harbinger Publications.

Horney, K. (1937). The Neurotic Personality in Our Time. N.Y.: W.W. Norton.

Hyman, B.M. & Pedrick, C. (2005). The OCD Workbook. 2nd ed. Oakland, CA: New Harbinger Publications.

Jowit, J. (2018). "What Is Depression and Why Is It Rising?" The Guardian, June 4.

Lambert, K. (2008). Lifting Depression. N.Y.: Basic Books.

Lancer, D. (2014). Conquering Shame and Codependency. Center City, Mn. Hazelden Publishing.

Lancer, D. (2015). Codependency for Dummies. Hoboken, N.J.: John Wiley & Sons.

Leahy, R. (2005). The Worry Cure. N.Y. : Harmony Books.

Lennick, D. & Kiel, F. (2008). Moral Intelligence. Upper Saddle River, N.J.: Pearson.

Marcia, J. et. al. (1993). Ego Identity. N.Y.: Springer- Verlag.

McGonigal, K. (2012). The Willpower Instinct. N.Y. : Avery

McQuaid, J & Carmona, P. (2004). Peaceful Mind. Oakland, CA.: New Harbinger Publications.

Moore, C. (2014). The Resilience Break-Through. Austin, Texas: Greenleaf

Neenan, M. (2011). Developing Resilience. N.Y.: Routledge.

O'Connor, R. (2010). Undoing Depression. N.Y.: Little, Brown & Company

O'Hanlon, B. (2014). Out of The Blue. N.Y.: W.W. Norton.

Orloff, J. (2009). Emotional Freedom. N.Y.: Harmony Books.

Paterson, R. (2000). The Assertiveness Workbook. Oakland, CA: New Harbinger Publications.

Reivich, K. & Shatte, A. (2002). The Resilience Factor. N.Y.: Broadway Books.

Rendon, J. (2015). Upside: The New Science of Posttraumatic Growth. N.Y.: Touchstone.

Riesman, David (2001). The Lonely Crowd. Rev. Ed. New Haven, CT.: Yale Nota Bene Books

Rosenbloom, D. (2010). Life After Trauma. N.Y.: Guilford Press.

Rothbaum, B. (2006). Pathological Anxiety. N.Y.: Guilford Press.

Schiraldi, G. (2001). The Self-Esteem Workbook. Oakland, CA: New Harbinger Publications, Inc.

Scioli, A & Biller, H. (2010). The Power of Hope. N.Y.: Health Communications, Inc.

Segerstrom, S.C. (2006). Breaking Murphy's Law. N.Y.: Guilford Press.

Toffler, A. (1970). Future Shock. N.Y.: Bantam Books

Toffler, A. (1980). The Third Wave. N.Y.: Bantam Books.

Viscott, D. (1996). Emotional Resilience. N.Y.: Three Rivers Press.

Walker, L. (2017). Battered Woman Syndrome. 4th ed. N.Y.: Springer Publishing Company.

Yalom, I. (1980). Existential Psychotherapy. N.Y.: Basic Books.

Yatham, L. & Kusumakar, V. (2009). Eds. Bipolar Disorder. 2nd. ed. N.Y.: Taylor & Francis Group.

About the Author

Joe S. Bean, Ph.D. has functioned as a licensed Ph.D. psychotherapist since 2003. After receiving his Ph.D. in the field of psychology, he worked in college settings for many years and achieved the rank of Associate Professor of Psychology before he established his private counseling practice.

Printed in the United States
By Bookmasters